EVERYDAY FORMS

GLOBE FEARON
EDUCATIONAL PUBLISHER
PARAMUS, NEW JERSEY

Paramount Publishing

Reviewers:

Doris A. Baker
Adult Basic Education
Dallas Independent School District
Dallas, Texas

Janie Bonham
Paris Junior College
Paris, Texas

Valeria A. Cooke
Adult and Community Education
Victoria, Texas

Henrietta Coursey,
Coordinator, Staff Development
for Basic Education and
Computer Technology
New York City Public Schools
Office of Adult and
  Continuing Education
Brooklyn, New York

Charles Gross
Lindsey Hopkins Technical Education Center
Miami, Florida

Renée B. Klosz
Lindsey Hopkins Technical Education Center
Miami, Florida

Jesse Nix
Beaumont Independent School District
Beaumont, Texas

Nancy Olds, Facilitator for ABE
New Haven Adult and Continuing Education
New Haven, Connecticut

Credits:

Editorial Development: VADAM
  Publishers, Inc.
Project Director: Mark Moscowitz
Writer: Roberta Mantus
Editor: Olive Collen
Copyeditor: Susan K. Tatiner
Keyboarder: Mary Ann Fleming
Proofreader: J. Dennis Papp

Production Manager: Penny Gibson
Production Editor: Walt Niedner
Art Director: Nancy Sharkey
Interior Design: Keithley Associates
Electronic Manuscript Management:
  Keithley Associates
Electronic Illustration: Keithley Associates

Copyright © 1994 by Globe Fearon Educational Publisher, 240 Frisch Court, Paramus, New Jersey 07652. All rights reserved. No part of this book may be reproduced or transmitted in any form or by any means, electrical or mechanical, including photocopying, recording, or by any information storage and retrieval system, without permission in writing from the publisher.

Printed in the United States of America. 1 2 3 4 5 6 7 8 9 10   96 95 94 93

ISBN 835-90698-1

GLOBE FEARON
EDUCATIONAL PUBLISHER
PARAMUS, NEW JERSEY

Paramount Publishing

CONTENTS

To the Student   iv

▶ **Chapter 1**   School and Job-Related Forms   1

Lesson 1	School Application	2
Lesson 2	Job Application	6
Lesson 3	Employee's Withholding Allowance Certificate (W-4)	11
Lesson 4	Employment Eligibility Verification	15
Lesson 5	Civil Service Test Application	19

▶ **Chapter 2**   Bank Forms   23

Lesson 6	Application for Savings Account	24
Lesson 7	Application for Checking Account	28
Lesson 8	Bank Deposit	32
Lesson 9	Withdrawal from Savings	34
Lesson 10	Checks and Check Register	37
Lesson 11	Check Endorsement	44
Lesson 12	Bank Statement Reconciliation	47
Lesson 13	Application for Car Loan	53

▶ **Chapter 3**   Medical Forms   57

Lesson 14	Medical History	58
Lesson 15	Application for Medicaid	61
Lesson 16	Medical Insurance Claim	72

▶ **Chapter 4**   Postal Forms   77

Lesson 17	Receipt for Insured Mail	78
Lesson 18	Postal Money Order	81
Lesson 19	Express Mail	83
Lesson 20	Return Receipt	86

▶ **Chapter 5**   Consumer Forms   89

Lesson 21	Bank Credit Card Application	90
Lesson 22	Department Store Credit Card Application	94
Lesson 23	Life Insurance Application	98
Lesson 24	Lease	106

▶ **Chapter 6**   Government Forms   109

Lesson 25	Application for Driver's License	110
Lesson 26	Application for Marriage License	116
Lesson 27	Application for Social Security Card	119
Lesson 28	Application for Passport	123
Lesson 29	Voter Registration	129
Lesson 30	Income Tax Return (Form 1040EZ)	133

TO THE STUDENT

It is almost impossible to get through life without ever having to fill out a form. We are faced with forms every day—at work, at the bank, at the post office, as consumers, and as citizens. People often feel uncomfortable about filling out forms. Some forms may have difficult words. Some may be very long. Others may look very hard to fill out. You can become more at ease about filling out forms by practicing how to fill them out.

This book is divided into 6 chapters and 30 lessons. Each lesson contains a different kind of form. There are forms you will find at work or at school, bank forms, medical forms, postal forms, consumer forms, and government forms.

<u>Note</u>: **Some forms ask for personal information. If you do not want to use your own personal information in filling out the forms in this book, you can make something up, or you can leave some lines blank.**

GENERAL HINTS

The following list offers hints on how to approach filling out all forms. These are not mentioned in the lessons, so this is the only place you will find this advice. You should follow it when you fill out the forms in this book, as well as the forms you may be faced with in real life.

❶ **Print your answers.** Many forms will have this instruction printed on them. Even if a form does not tell you to print, you should print everything but your signature on every form. In this book, when you are told to "write" something, this means that you should print.

❷ **Use a ballpoint pen.** Many forms come with their own copies. For example, three copies of one form may be joined together. You will fill out the top sheet. The two copies under the top sheet will be filled out automatically as you write. You must press hard with the pen to make sure that your writing prints on all three copies. Ballpoint pens are the best pens to use when you must press hard. Also, ink from other kinds of pens can smudge or be fuzzy. This usually does not happen with ballpoint pens.

❸ **Use blue or black ink.** Blue and black inks are the easiest to read. Also, they do not look unusual or stand out in any way. Red and green inks are harder to read and look less acceptable than blue or black.

❹ **Follow instructions.** Most forms have instructions printed on them. Be sure that you understand the instructions before you fill out the form.

❺ **Read before you write.** People often make mistakes when filling out forms because they do not look ahead to see the next question or the next line of a question. If you know what is coming, you will be less likely to make a mistake. So be sure to read a form before you fill it out.

❻ **Ask questions.** You may find a question on a form that you do not understand or that you are not sure how to answer. In most cases, you will be giving the form to someone in person. If so, leave the question blank and ask for help. Then go back and answer the question.

CHAPTER 1

SCHOOL AND JOB-RELATED FORMS

All the forms in this chapter relate to important life decisions that affect your future. Filling out a school application is the first step toward helping you get a good job. Filling out a job application means that you are ready to start a new job. You must fill out the two government forms—the W-4 and the immigration form—when you start a job. The application for the civil service is another kind of job application. It is for a job working for the government.

LESSON 1

School Application

There are lots of reasons why adults go to school. They may want to complete their high school education, get job training, help their chances of getting a promotion on a job, or get a college degree. Sometimes, people take classes just because they are interested in learning.

Whatever the reason, there are many different kinds of schools that can help people achieve their goals. Some are public colleges or community colleges that are run by local or state governments. Others are private schools. Some schools offer classes during the day. Others offer them at night.

Also, schools or local community organizations, such as the YMCA, offer classes for adults. Students are not graded in these classes, and they do not receive diplomas or degrees from the schools.

▶ *Be Prepared*

You should make several decisions before you go back to school. You should have an idea of what you want to study and what you want to get out of the classes you attend. You should also decide whether you want to take a full course of study that leads to a diploma, certificate, or degree. Maybe you want to attend a few classes to learn about a subject that may help you in your work. Or you may want to learn about something that is of interest to you personally.

You should think about how much time you are willing to spend attending classes and studying. You should also think about how much time a course of study will take. For example, to get an associate's degree from a community college usually takes two years going full time during the day. It takes longer if you attend night classes only. Private business or trade schools offer courses that can last as long as a year or more. Some courses in these schools are for 10 to 12 weeks, however.

You can find out what different schools have to offer and what classes are available by reviewing school catalogs. You can get a school catalog by phoning or writing to a school. Check in the yellow pages of the phone book to find out about different schools in your area. Or call schools you may already know about.

Before you fill out a school application, you should know what course of study you want to take, since many applications will ask you this question.

School applications also ask you about your educational background. You should know, for example, what year you received your high school diploma and the names of other schools you have attended.

Before you decide to attend a school, find out what your financial responsibilities will be. Some schools require that you pay a fee when you submit an application. Others do not. Some schools accept major credit cards as payment. Others do not. The cost of going to school varies greatly. Some schools help you arrange for financial assistance from government funding.

Learn as much as you can about a school before you decide to attend.

School Application Vocabulary

certify   State as being true.

course of study   An area of focus in education, such as secretarial or mechanical.

Tests of General Educational Development (GED)   A certificate stating that someone has completed the requirements for graduating from high school. A GED is obtained in some way other than the usual four-year high school program.

program   Same as course of study.

How to Fill Out the Application

The school application in this lesson is for a private business and technical school. The following hints will help you fill out the application. The numbers in the following list match the circled numbers on the school application. Some parts of the application do not have circled numbers. You should be able to fill in these parts of the form without any special hints or explanation.

1. Write your full name here (first, middle name or initial, and last).

2. Write your telephone number. Write the area code between the parentheses.

3. Write your street address on the first line, and write the city, state, and zip code on the second line.

4. Write your date of birth all in numbers. For example, if you were born on February 13, 1965, you would write "2/13/65".

5. Answer this question by writing "yes" or "no" on the line.

6. If you are interested in a business program, check the one you want to study. Do not check anything under the trade/technical program. If you are interested in a trade/technical program, check the one you want to study. Do not check anything under the business program.

Lane Business and Technical School

Student Information

① Name _____ Telephone no. _____ ②

③ Address _____
_____

④ Date of birth _____ Male _____ Female _____

Social security no. _____ Do you have a driver's license? _____ ⑤

Program — Business

Check the program in which you are interested.

⑥
- ☐ Administrative Assistant
- ☐ Marketing
- ☐ Travel and Tourism
- ☐ Accounting
- ☐ Clerical / Receptionist
- ☐ Computer Programming
- ☐ Fashion Design
- ☐ Word Processing
- ☐ Management

Program — Trade / Technicial

Check the program in which you are interested.

⑥
- ☐ Automotive Mechanics
- ☐ Truck Driving
- ☐ Computer Repair
- ☐ Diesel Truck Mechanics
- ☐ Refrigeration / Air-Conditioning Repair
- ☐ TV Repair
- ☐ Drafting
- ☐ Welding

Education

⑦ High school _____

⑧ Check the highest grade you completed. ☐ 9 ☐ 10 ☐ 11 ☐ 12

⑨ Did you graduate? _____ Year _____ ⑩

⑪ If you did not graduate, have you obtained a high-school equivalency diploma or a GED? _____ Year _____ ⑫

⑬ College _____

⑭ Did you graduate? _____ Year _____ ⑮ If not, how many years did you complete? _____ ⑯

Other

⑰ Name of school _____

Course of study _____ Did you graduate? _____ Year _____

I certify that the above information is complete and accurate.

⑱ Signature _____ Date _____

4 CHAPTER 1 SCHOOL AND JOB-RELATED FORMS

7. Write the name of the high school you attended.

8. Check the highest grade you finished in high school. If you started but did not finish a grade, do not check that year. For example, if you started but did not finish the 12th grade, check the 11th grade as the highest grade you completed.

9. Answer yes or no.

10. If you graduated from high school, write the year you graduated. If you did not graduate, do not write anything.

11. Answer yes or no.

12. If you have a high-school equivalency diploma or a GED certificate, write the year you received it.

13. If you attended college, write the name of the college.

14. Write yes or no.

15. If you graduated from college, write the year you graduated.

16. Write the total number of years you completed in college. For example, if you completed your second year and left before or during your third year, write "2."

17. If you have ever attended any other school for the purpose of graduating (not just to take a course or two), write the name of the school.

18. When you sign (not print) your name, you are stating that all the information you have provided in the application is true.

Fill Out the Application

Review the programs you can study at the Lane Business and Technical School. Select one that is of interest to you (even if you do not plan to attend this kind of school or study any of the subjects listed). Then fill out the application, using your own personal and educational information.

LESSON 2

Job Application

A job application is a form that you will be asked to fill out when you apply for a job. Every company has its own job application, so the forms differ from one place to the next. However, all job applications are alike in some ways. Job applications always ask for the names of other companies you worked for and the kinds of jobs you had at those places. They also always ask for information about your education, such as the names and addresses of schools you attended.

Applications sometimes ask for references, who are people who know you and can tell the company about you. A reference might be a teacher or a friend.

▶ Be Prepared

You will usually fill out a job application while you are waiting for someone from the company to talk to you. So you will have to bring information with you when you apply for a job. This should include the correct names, addresses (including zip codes), and telephone numbers of companies you worked for in the past. If you have a job now and are looking for a new one, be sure you have this information about the company you are working for. Also have the names and job titles of the people you have worked for.

You should have the names and addresses of schools you attended. And you should have handy a list of references, with names, addresses, and telephone numbers. You should never use people as references without asking their permission first.

Job Application Vocabulary

account for   Explain.

applicant   A person applying for a job.

certificate   An official paper stating qualifications or skills.

certify   State as being true.

foregoing   Mentioned before.

misrepresentation   Something that is false or misleading.

proficient   Skilled or expert at something.

qualifications   Qualities or skills.

rejection   Refusal to accept.

relocate   Move to another place.

▶ How to Fill Out the Application

The following hints will help you fill out the job application shown on the next two pages. The numbers in the following list match the circled numbers on the job application. Some parts of the application do not have circled numbers. You should be able to fill in these parts of the form without any special hints or explanation.

PAGE 1

1. Fill in your name and permanent address. If you do not have a temporary address, draw a small line in the box. This shows that you read this part of the form but that it does not apply to you. Include your area code with your phone number.

2. Write the title of the job you want. If you do not know the exact title, it is OK to write something general, such as loading dock worker or office clerk.

3. You should put down a range for the salary you want, for example, $300 to $350 a week. Or, instead of a weekly salary, you can put a yearly, monthly, or hourly salary.

4. Check one of the boxes here to show whether you are interested in a permanent or temporary job and whether you want a part-time job.

5. Write the date you can begin working for this company. This can be a specific date (a month and day), or it can be an estimate, such as June. If you now have a job, you should expect that you will not be able to start a new job until you have given notice at your present one. When you give notice, you tell your supervisor the date you plan to leave. Usually people give employers two weeks' notice. So the date you could start a new job would be two weeks after you give notice.

6. Some companies have branches or plants in lots of places. This company is asking whether you would be willing to move to another city or state.

7. Write here any kind of equipment or machine that you know how to operate in your work. This could be a lathe, a calculator, a switchboard, or some other piece of equipment.

8. This question asks about any special qualifications, licenses, or certificates you might have. For example, you might have a cosmetology or plumbing license. Or you could have a special skill in bookkeeping.

9. This question is about computers and software. Write here the kind of computer you know how to operate and the name of the software you know how to use.

D&L Products

APPLICATION FOR EMPLOYMENT
An Equal Opportunity Employer

Please PRINT answers to all questions.

DATE OF APPLICATION

1 PERSONAL DATA

NAME OF APPLICANT (*Last, first, middle*)	CITIZEN OF U.S.A.? ☐ YES ☐ NO	SOCIAL SECURITY NO.
PERMANENT ADDRESS (*Street, city, state, zip*)		PHONE NO.
TEMPORARY ADDRESS (*Street, city, state, zip*)		PHONE NO.

CHECK APPROPRIATE BOX FOR AGE: UNDER 16 ☐ , 16 OR 17 ☐ , 18 THROUGH 69 ☐ , 70 OR OVER ☐

TYPE OF WORK

2 JOB WANTED

3 SALARY DESIRED

4 WORK TO BE ☐ PERMANENT ☐ TEMPORARY ☐ PART-TIME

5 DATE AVAILABLE FOR WORK

6 ARE YOU WILLING TO RELOCATE? ☐ YES ☐ NO

7 WHAT JOB-RELATED EQUIPMENT OR MACHINES DO YOU OPERATE?

8 WHAT SPECIAL QUALIFICATIONS, LICENSES, OR CERTIFICATES DO YOU POSSESS?

9 DO YOU OPERATE A COMPUTER? ☐ YES ☐ NO   WHAT KIND?

WHAT SOFTWARE ARE YOU PROFICIENT IN?

10 EDUCATION

SCHOOL	NAME AND LOCATION	NUMBER OF YEARS ATTENDED	DIPLOMA OR DEGREE YES / NO	HIGHEST GRADE COMPLETED FOR EACH (1, 2, ETC.)	TYPE OF COURSE
GRADE					
HIGH					
COLLEGE OR BUSINESS					
OTHER					

11 EMERGENCY

IN CASE OF EMERGENCY NOTIFY (*Name*)	PHONE NO.
ADDRESS (*Street, city, state, zip*)	

Page 1 of job application

Complete employment record and work history. Please account for the time since leaving school. List month and year employed starting with last place of employment. If unemployed, give dates and explain why.

12 EMPLOYMENT HISTORY

EMPLOYED FROM	TO	COMPANY AND ADDRESS *(Street, city, state, zip)*	POSITION OR TYPE OF WORK	SALARY OR WAGE	REASON FOR LEAVING

13 REFERENCES

List at least two persons well acquainted with you but not relatives or former employers.

NAME	OCCUPATION	ADDRESS	PHONE NO.

RELATIVE OR FRIEND EMPLOYED BY THIS COMPANY	DEPARTMENT

14 MILITARY SERVICE

ARE YOU A VETERAN? ☐ YES ☐ NO	BRANCH OF MIILITARY SERVICE	PERIOD OF SERVICE
RANKED ATTAINED	MILITARY SPECIALTY	

15 APPLICANT'S STATEMENT AND AGREEMENT

READ THE FOLLOWING CAREFULLY BEFORE SIGNING THIS APPLICATION FOR EMPLOYMENT.

1. I hereby certify that the foregoing answers are correct to the best of my knowledge and belief, and understand that misrepresentation in this application will be cause for rejection or dismissal.
2. If employed, I agree to conform to the rules and regulations governing employees and to use such safety devices and equipment as provided by the company.

_____ _____
DATE   SIGNATURE OF APPLICANT

16 PROCESSING

Applicant is not to write in the following spaces.

BY	DATE	ACTION	RESULTS
		APPLICATION REVIEW	
		TEST	
		INTERVIEW (1)	
		INTERVIEW (2)	
		REFERENCE CHECK	
		MEDICAL	

DATE APPROVED FOR HIRE	SIGNATURE	TITLE

DATE TO START	DATE NOTIFIED	IF NOT HIRED, DATE NOTIFIED	SIGNATURE

Page 2 of job application

10. This section of the application is about your education from grade school on. The second from the last column at the right asks how much schooling you completed. For example, if you graduated from high school, you completed through grade 12. If you did not graduate, write the grade you completed, such as grade 11 or 10. In the last column at the right, fill in whether you took academic, business, or general courses in high school. Also write in other kinds of courses you took if you continued your education.

11. If the company hires you, it will keep your application in its files. If you are hurt or become sick on the job, someone in the company will have to get in touch with someone who knows you. In this place on the form, write the name, address, and daytime phone number of the person you would want the company to contact in case of emergency.

PAGE 2

12. In the employment history part of the form, list your job, starting with the most recent one first. Then work your way back. The last column at the right asks for your reasons for leaving your previous jobs. If you were laid off or wanted better working conditions or a higher salary, it is OK to say so. If you were fired, it would be best to think of a way to say this that does not put you in a bad light. For example, you can say that you were terminated. People who are terminated lose their jobs but for many different reasons.

13. This is where the company asks for your references. Notice that on this application, the company does not want you to list relatives or people you worked for.

14. If you served in the military, provide the information requested. If you did not, check the No box and leave the rest of the questions blank.

15. This section is the only part of the form that does not require you to print your answers. You should read the statement, which says that the information you have provided is the truth, and then sign your name.

16. The last section of the form is for the company's use. You should not write in this section.

Fill Out the Application

Look over the application and then gather all the information you will need to fill it out. You can now fill out the form. If you are not looking for a job now, you can fill it out for a job that you would like to have in the future. If you are not sure about job titles or salaries, you can look in the want ads of a newspaper for examples.

LESSON 3

Employee's Withholding Allowance Certificate (W-4)

When you are hired for any job, you must fill out a form called an Employee's Withholding Allowance Certificate before you begin working. This form is often referred to as a W-4 form (or Form W-4). Your employer uses the information you write on the form to deduct the right amount of federal taxes from your paycheck.

The amount of money deducted from your paycheck depends on how much you earn and on the number of allowances (sometimes called **deductions** or **exemptions**) you take. The number of people, including yourself, who are dependent on you financially are allowances the government gives you. So an **allowance** is an amount of money per person that is not taxed. The more allowances you have, the less money is taken out of your paycheck.

▸ ## Be Prepared

Before you fill out the W-4 form, review your tax return from last year to see who is considered a dependent by the government and how many dependents you claimed. You may also want to talk to other working members of your household to find out their incomes so that you can tell whether you can claim them as dependents.

Employee's Withholding Allowance Certificate Vocabulary

allowance An amount of nontaxable money. An allowance is for you and the people who are financially dependent on you. Also called a deduction or an exemption.

exemption from withholding Not required to have tax money withheld from salary.

perjury Swearing to something that is not true.

spouse Husband or wife.

▸ ## How to Fill Out the Form

The following hints will help you fill out Form W-4. The numbers in the following list match the circled numbers on the form. Some parts of the form do not have circled numbers. You should be able to fill in these parts of the form without any special hints or explanation.

1. You can check one of three boxes. Check the first box if you are single. You can also check the first box if you are married but separated or if your spouse does not live in the United States. Check the second box if you are married.

   Check the third box if you are married but you want more money to be taken out of your taxes, as if you were single.

2. The name you fill in on this form must be the same as the name on your social security card. If the names are different, call the telephone number shown and check the box.

3. Before you can fill in the information here, you must fill out the worksheet part of the form.

A Enter "1" for **yourself** if no one else can claim you as a dependent . . . . A _____

B Enter "1" if:
- You are single and have only one job; or
- You are married, have only one job, and your spouse does not work; or
- Your wages from a second job or your spouse's wages (or the total of both) are $1,000 or less. . . B _____

C Enter "1" for your **spouse**. But, you may choose to enter -0- if you are married and have either a working spouse or more than one job (this may help you avoid having too little tax withheld) . . . . C _____

D Enter number of **dependents** (other than your spouse or yourself) whom you will claim on your tax return . . . D _____

E Enter "1" if you will file as **head of household** on your tax return (see conditions under "Head of Household," above) . E _____

F Enter "1" if you have at least $1,500 of **child or dependent care expenses** for which you plan to claim a credit . . F _____

G Add lines A through F and enter total here. **Note:** *This amount may be different from the number of exemptions you claim on your return* ▶ G _____

Worksheet part of Form W-4

The worksheet lists items A to G. Read each of these items carefully before you write your answer in the right-hand column. Let's look at items A to G more closely.

A. You can claim yourself as one dependent. Write "1" unless someone else claims you as a deduction.

B. There are three possible reasons why you can write a 1 here:
- The first is if you are not married and have only one job.
- The second is if you are married, have one job, and your spouse does not work.
- The third is if your wages from a second job or your spouse's wages are $1,000 or less for the whole year.

If any of these three reasons applies to you, write a "1" on the line at the right for B.

C. Write a "1" for the allowance if your spouse does not work. You can decide to write a "0" (zero) instead of a "1" if your spouse works or if you have more than one job. Remember that the more deductions you have, the less money is taken out of your paycheck in taxes. If you use this allowance now, you may have to pay more taxes when you file your tax return.

D. This is where a review of your tax return from last year will be helpful. Check to see how many dependents you claimed other than yourself and your spouse. For example, your dependents could include your children.

E. If you are the "head of household," write a "1" on the line at the right. Here is the government's explanation of a head of household:

> **Head of Household.** Generally, you may claim head of household filing status on your tax return only if you are unmarried and pay more than 50% of the costs of keeping up a home for yourself and your dependent(s) or other qualifying individuals.

F. If you think you will have nontaxable expenses for a dependent of $1,500 or more, write a "1" here. For example, some medical expenses are nontaxable expenses. If you are not sure about this, check your tax return from last year or do not write anything. Your taxes can be adjusted when you file your return.

G. Now add up all the 1s that you have written and write the total on the line at the right. This does not have to be the same number of allowances you took on your tax return last year.

Once you have completed the worksheet, go back to the W-4 form. Write your total number of allowances on the line next to the circled number 3. This should be the same number you wrote in item G on the worksheet.

4. If you want any more money deducted from your paycheck, write the amount here.

Form W-4.

LESSON 3　EMPLOYEE'S WITHHOLDING ALLOWANCE CERTIFICATE (W-4)　13

5. Sometimes, people have no money deducted from their paychecks for taxes. There are three reasons for this shown on the form. If no money will be deducted from your paycheck for taxes, all three reasons have to apply to you. The first reason is that all the taxes you paid last year were refunded, and you do not owe the government any tax money. The second is that you expect that you will have all your taxes refunded this year, and you will not owe the government any tax money. The third is that you expect to earn more than $600 this year, and you are not claimed as a dependent on someone else's taxes.

If you are not sure whether this applies to you, you can leave it blank. If you are not supposed to pay any taxes, the money you pay in will be returned to you.

6. When you sign this form, you are swearing that the information you provided is true.

7. Do not write here. The company fills out this part of the form.

Fill Out the Form

Assume that you have been hired for a new job. You have been asked to fill out a Form W-4. Use your own personal information and fill out the form.

LESSON 4

Employment Eligibility Verification

When you start working, your employer will ask you to fill out two forms that are required by the federal government. One is the W-4 form, which was covered in Lesson 3. The W-4 form relates to income taxes. The other form is the Employment Eligibility Verification form. This is required to prove that you are legally allowed to work in the United States. Only citizens of the United States or aliens who are permanent residents or who have special approval can work in this country.

▶ *Be Prepared*

The Employment Eligibility Verification form is divided into three parts. You must fill out the first part. Your employer will fill out the second and third parts. Therefore, you will not write very much on this form. However, you must bring documents that prove your identity and your eligibility to work and show them to your employer. A list of these documents is given on the back of the form and is shown on page 17.

As you can see, there are three lists. If you have a document from list A, you do not have to provide anything else. If you do not have any of the documents named in list A, you must provide one document from list B and one document from list C.

Before you start work, you should make sure that you have the documents you will need to complete the Employment Eligibility Verification form.

Employment Eligibility Verification Form Vocabulary

discrimination   Prejudiced action or treatment.

eligibility   The condition of meeting requirements for approval.

expiration   The point at which something ends.

maiden name   A woman's last name before she was married.

perjury   The act of swearing to something that is not true.

verification   Proof of truth or accuracy.

▶ *How to Fill Out the Form*

The following hints will help you fill out the form. The numbers in the following list match the circled numbers on the form. Some parts of the form do not have circled numbers. You should be able to fill in these

LESSON 4   EMPLOYMENT ELIGIBILITY VERIFICATION   **15**

parts of the form without any special hints or explanation. You are supposed to fill out only section 1 of this form. Do not write in sections 2 or 3.

1. If you are a married woman and you changed your name when you got married, write your maiden name here. If you are a man or a woman whose name has never been changed, do not write anything in this box.

2. Write your birth date all in numbers. For example, if you were born on June 12, 1972, you would write "6/12/72." Notice that after the words *Date of Birth*, the words *month/day/year* are shown. The slashes (/) between the words are used to tell you that the date should be written all in numbers, with slashes between the numbers.

3. Check the box that applies to you.

4. When you write your name here, you are swearing that the information you have written on the form is true. You are also swearing that the documents you have provided for proof of identity and employment eligibility are not false.

5. Write today's date all in numbers, the way you wrote your birth date.

6. In some cases, someone else fills out section 1 for the person applying for a job. If this happens, the person who filled out section 1 has to write in this part of the form.

Fill Out the Form

Using your own personal information, turn to page 18 and fill out section 1 of the form now.

LISTS OF ACCEPTABLE DOCUMENTS

LIST A

Documents that Establish Both Identity and Employment Eligibility

1. U.S. Passport (unexpired or expired)

2. Certificate of U.S. Citizenship (INS Form N-560 or N-561)

3. Certificate of Naturalization (INS Form N-550 or N-570)

4. Unexpired foreign passport, with *I-551 stamp or* attached INS Form I-94 indicating unexpired employment authorization

5. Alien Registration Receipt Card with photograph (INS Form I-151 or I-551)

6. Unexpired Temporary Resident Card (INS Form I-688)

7. Unexpired Employment Authorization Card (INS Form I-688A)

8. Unexpired Reentry Permit (INS Form I-327)

9. Unexpired Refugee Travel Document (INS Form I-571)

10. Unexpired Employment Authorization Document issued by the INS which contains a photograph (INS Form I-688B)

OR

LIST B

Documents that Establish Identity

1. Driver's license or ID card issued by a state or outlying possession of the United States provided it contains a photograph or information such as name, date of birth, sex, height, eye color, and address

2. ID card issued by federal, state, or local government agencies or entities provided it contains a photograph or information such as name, date of birth, sex, height, eye color. and address

3. School ID card with a photograph

4. Voter's registration card

5. U.S. Military card or draft record

6. Military dependent's ID card

7. U.S. Coast Guard Merchant Mariner Card

8. Native American tribal document

9. Driver's license issued by a Canadian government authority

For persons under age 18 who are unable to present a document listed above:

10. School record or report card

11. Clinic, doctor, or hospital record

12. Day-care or nursery school record

AND

LIST C

Documents that Establish Employment Eligibility

1. U.S. social security card issued by the Social Security Administration *(other than a card stating it is not valid for employment)*

2. Certification of Birth Abroad issued by the Department of State *(Form FS-545 or Form DS-1350)*

3. Original or certified copy of a birth certificate issued by a state, county, municipal authority or outlying possession of the United States bearing an official seal

4. Native American tribal document

5. U.S. Citizen ID Card *(INS Form I-197)*

6. ID Card for use of Resident Citizen in the United States *(INS Form I-179)*

7. Unexpired employment authorization document issued by the INS *(other than those listed under List A)*

U.S. Department of Justice
Immigration and Naturalization Service

OMB No. 1115-0136
Employment Eligibility Verification

Please read instructions carefully before completing this form. The instructions must be available during completion of this form. ANTI-DISCRIMINATION NOTICE. It is illegal to discriminate against work eligible individuals. Employers CANNOT specify which document(s) they will accept from an employee. The refusal to hire an individual because of a future expiration date may also constitute illegal discrimination.

Section 1. Employee Information and Verification. *To be completed and signed by employee at the time employment begins*

Print Name: Last	First	Middle Initial	Maiden Name

Address *(Street Name and Number)*	Apt. #	Date of Birth *(month/day/year)*

City	State	Zip Code	Social Security #

I am aware that federal law provides for imprisonment and/or fines for false statements or use of false documents in connection with the completion of this form.

I attest, under penalty of perjury, that I am (check one of the following):
☐ A citizen or national of the United States
☐ A Lawful Permanent Resident (Alien # A _____)
☐ An alien authorized to work until ___/___/___
(Alien # or Admission # _____)

Employee's Signature | Date *(month/day/year)*

Preparer and/or Translator Certification. *(To be completed and signed if Section 1 is prepared by a person other than the employee.) I attest, under penalty of perjury, that I have assisted in the completion of this form and that to the best of my knowledge the information is true and correct.*

Preparer's/Translator's Signature | Print Name

Address *(Street Name and Number, City, State, Zip Code)* | Date *(month/day/year)*

Section 2. Employer Information and Verification. *To be completed and signed by employer.* **Examine one document from List A OR examine one document from List B and one from List C** as listed on the reverse of the form and record the title, number and expiration date, if any, of the document(s)

List A	OR	List B	AND	List C
Document title:				
Issuing authority:				
Document #:				
Expiration Date (if any): ___/___/___		___/___/___		___/___/___
Document #:				
Expiration Date (if any): ___/___/___				

CERTIFICATION - I attest, under penalty of perjury, that I have examined the document(s) presented by the above-named employee, that the above-listed document(s) appear to be genuine and to relate to the employee named, that the employee began employment on *(month/day/year)* ___/___/___ and that to the best of my knowledge the employee is eligible to work in the United States. (State employment agencies may omit the date the employee began employment).

Signature of Employer or Authorized Representative	Print Name	Title

Business or Organization Name	Address *(Street Name and Number, City, State, Zip Code)*	Date *(month/day/year)*

Section 3. Updating and Reverification. *To be completed and signed by employer*

A. New Name *(if applicable)*	B. Date of rehire *(month/day/year) (if applicable)*

C. If employee's previous grant of work authorization has expired, provide the information below for the document that establishes current employment eligibility.

Document title: _____ Document #: _____ Expiration Date (if any): ___/___/___

I attest, under penalty of perjury, that to the best of my knowledge, this employee is eligible to work in the United States, and if the employee presented document(s), the document(s) I have examined appear to be genuine and to relate to the individual.

Signature of Employer or Authorized Representative	Date *(month/day/year)*

LESSON 5

Civil Service Test Application

People who work for the local, state, or federal government have **civil service jobs**. Usually, civil service workers must be tested before they are hired. When people want to take civil service tests, they must apply by filling out forms.

For example, if you wanted to get a job with the postal service, first you would have to find out about the test from your local postmaster.

▶ Be Prepared

Different types of civil service jobs have different kinds of requirements. So the applications for the tests vary depending on the job. Before you apply to take the test, find out what the qualifications are for the job you want.

The application to take the test for a job with the U.S. Postal Service requires two things. First, you must know the name of the test you want to take. Second, you must know the name of the post office branch where you want to work.

The application is in two parts. You must fill in both parts and take them or mail them to your local postmaster. One part—the admission card—will be returned to you. Along with the admission card, you will receive sample questions from the test you will be taking, and you will also receive test instructions. You must bring the admission card with you when you take the test. You should also bring your identification.

Civil Service Test Application Vocabulary

separated under honorable conditions Received an honorable discharge from military service.

veteran preference Special attention given to people who have served in the U.S. armed forces and who meet certain qualifications.

▶ How to Fill Out the Civil Service Test Application

The two-part application card shown on the next two pages is to take the test for a civil service job with the U.S. Postal Service. The following hints will help you fill out the card. The numbers in the following list

LESSON 5   CIVIL SERVICE TEST APPLICATION   **19**

match the circled numbers on the card. Some parts of the card do not have circled numbers. You should be able to fill in these parts of the card without any special hints or explanation.

TEST APPLICATION CARD

1. Write your name in the order noted on the card. Write your last name, then your first name, and then the initial(s) of your middle name(s).

2. Write your date of birth all in numbers. For example, if you were born on September 23, 1970, you would write "9/23/70."

3. Write your telephone number, including the area code.

4. Write today's date all in numbers.

5. The name of the examination you want to take goes here.

6. Since this application is to take a test for a job with the post office, you should write here the branch of the post office at which you would like to work. This may be a branch close to where you live.

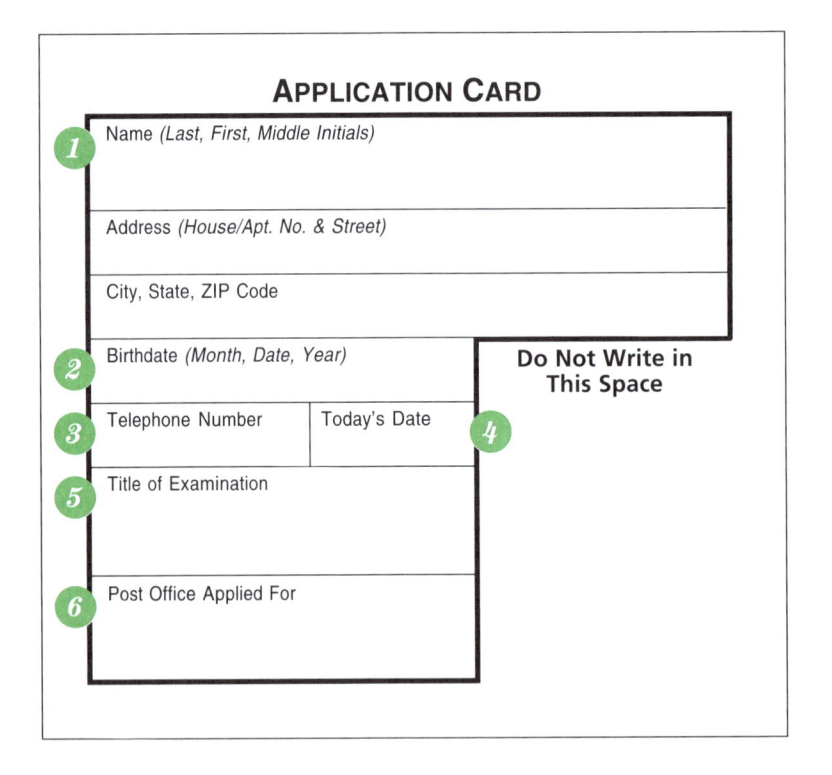

APPLICATION CARD

① Name *(Last, First, Middle Initials)*

Address *(House/Apt. No. & Street)*

City, State, ZIP Code

② Birthdate *(Month, Date, Year)*

Do Not Write in This Space

③ Telephone Number | Today's Date | ④

⑤ Title of Examination

⑥ Post Office Applied For

TEST ADMISSION CARD

7. The name of the examination you want to take goes here.

8. Write each number of your social security number in one of the boxes.

9. Write your date of birth all in numbers.

10. Write today's date all in numbers.

11. Write the name of the post office branch where you would like to work.

12. If you are a veteran of one of the branches of the military and you received an honorable discharge, fill in this part. Write the date you entered the service (all in numbers) after the word *From* and the date you left the service (also all in numbers) after *to*.

13. Many branches of the civil service give special treatment or attention to qualified veterans. If you do not qualify, check the No box. Then move on to the last part of the card, where you write your name and address.

If you want special veteran preference, check the Yes box. Then read the information that follows and check the box that applies to you.

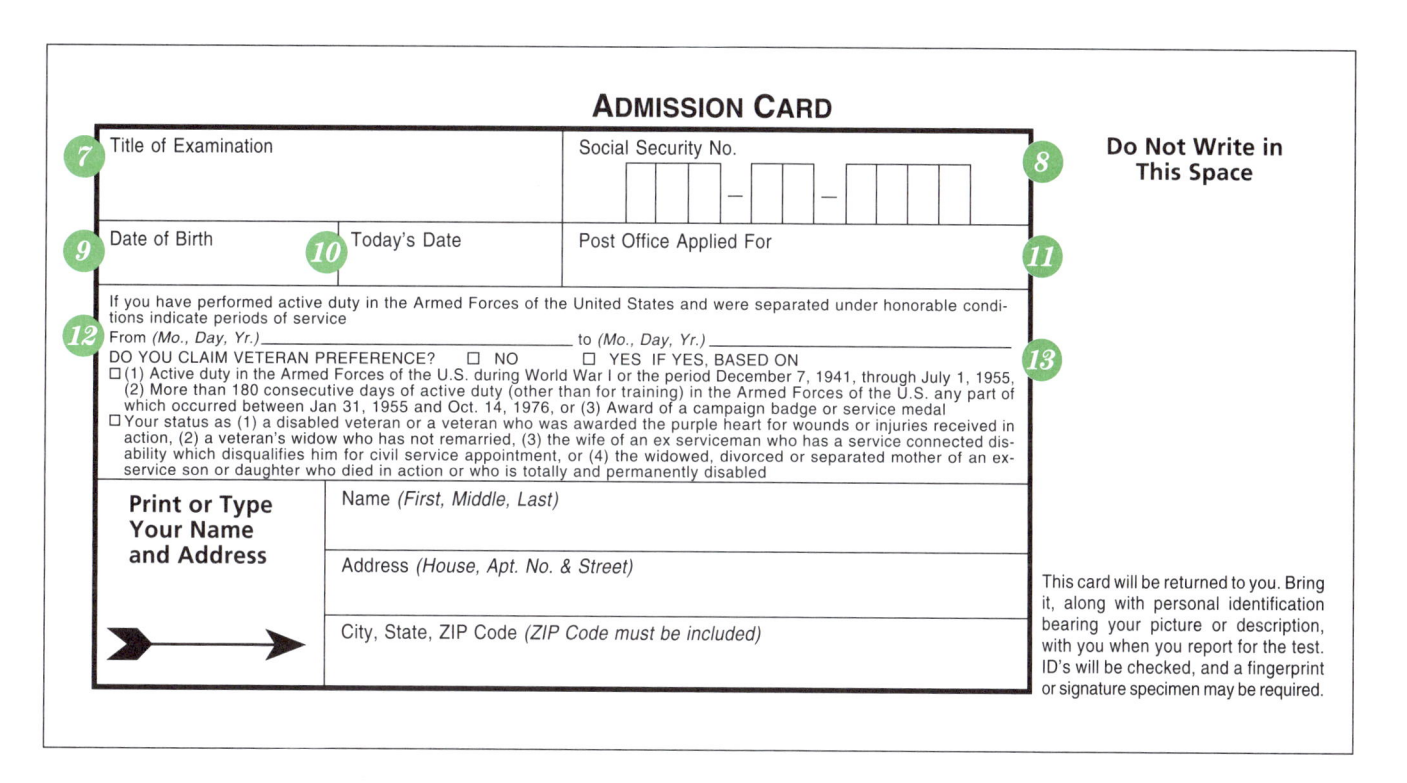

ADMISSION CARD

7 Title of Examination

Social Security No.

8 Do Not Write in This Space

9 Date of Birth

10 Today's Date

Post Office Applied For

11

If you have performed active duty in the Armed Forces of the United States and were separated under honorable conditions indicate periods of service

12 From *(Mo., Day, Yr.)* _____ to *(Mo., Day, Yr.)* _____

DO YOU CLAIM VETERAN PREFERENCE? ☐ NO   ☐ YES IF YES, BASED ON

☐ (1) Active duty in the Armed Forces of the U.S. during World War I or the period December 7, 1941, through July 1, 1955, (2) More than 180 consecutive days of active duty (other than for training) in the Armed Forces of the U.S. any part of which occurred between Jan 31, 1955 and Oct. 14, 1976, or (3) Award of a campaign badge or service medal

☐ Your status as (1) a disabled veteran or a veteran who was awarded the purple heart for wounds or injuries received in action, (2) a veteran's widow who has not remarried, (3) the wife of an ex serviceman who has a service connected disability which disqualifies him for civil service appointment, or (4) the widowed, divorced or separated mother of an exservice son or daughter who died in action or who is totally and permanently disabled

13

Print or Type Your Name and Address →

Name *(First, Middle, Last)*

Address *(House, Apt. No. & Street)*

City, State, ZIP Code *(ZIP Code must be included)*

This card will be returned to you. Bring it, along with personal identification bearing your picture or description, with you when you report for the test. ID's will be checked, and a fingerprint or signature specimen may be required.

Fill Out the Card

Using your own personal information, fill out both parts of the card. Leave the title of the examination blank. Select a post office branch that is near your home.

LESSON 5 CIVIL SERVICE TEST APPLICATION **21**

CHAPTER 2

BANK FORMS

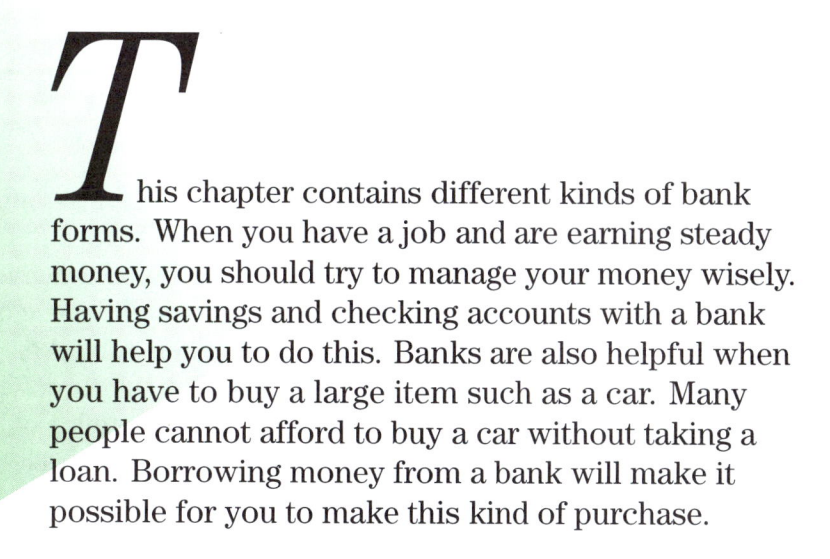

▲

This chapter contains different kinds of bank forms. When you have a job and are earning steady money, you should try to manage your money wisely. Having savings and checking accounts with a bank will help you to do this. Banks are also helpful when you have to buy a large item such as a car. Many people cannot afford to buy a car without taking a loan. Borrowing money from a bank will make it possible for you to make this kind of purchase.

LESSON 6

Application for Savings Account

You need the money you earn to pay for your housing, gas and electric, food, clothing, and entertainment. Even though you need your money to pay for these living expenses, it is a good idea to take some money from every paycheck and put it into a **savings account**. Money kept in savings accounts earns interest. This means that your money earns money, just by being deposited in a bank.

The interest earned is a percentage of the amount of money you have in the bank. The interest paid on savings accounts varies from bank to bank. It may be 4 to 7 percent per year.

You may think that you do not earn enough money to set aside money for a savings account. But only $5 a week in a savings account will be $260 plus interest by the end of one year. This would be enough for holiday shopping and maybe other holiday expenses. And $10 a week for a year will be $520 plus interest. This is enough money to go on vacation or buy a new color TV.

▶ Be Prepared

Just about anyone can open a savings account. Banks do not require any special information when you open a savings account. The application for a savings account shown in this book is called a **signature card**. The card asks for some basic information about you, and it asks for your signature. When you take money out of your account, you will need to show your signature. This means that when you want to withdraw money, the bank teller will match the signature you write with the signature on the card. As long as the signatures match, you will be given the money. The bank matches the signatures to protect your money. You can withdraw money only with your signature. You do not need to show a signature when you put money into your savings account.

Sometimes, people want joint savings accounts. This means that two or more people share an account. In this case, the people who share the account must each fill out the form, provide the information requested, and sign the card. Since people sharing an account must sign the card individually, you can go to the bank together to open the account or one person can take the card to the other person and have that person sign the card. When you bring the signed card back, the account can be opened.

The card requires basic information, so there is nothing special that you need to prepare for. However, you will be expected to deposit money when you open the account. This means that you will have to put money in the account to get it started. This does not have to be a lot of money.

Application for Savings Account Vocabulary

amendment   A change.

balance   The amount in a bank account.

collateral   Money or property that guarantees a loan. For example, if a person borrows money, using a car or a house as collateral, and cannot repay the loan, the person who loaned the money can take the car or the house in place of the money owed.

to endorse   To write one's name.

party   A person.

primary   First.

spouse   A husband or wife.

How to Fill Out the Application

The following list will help you fill out the application. The numbers in the following list match the circled numbers on the application. Some parts of the application do not have circled numbers. You should be able to fill in these parts of the application without any special hints or explanation.

FRONT OF SAVINGS ACCOUNT SIGNATURE CARD

1. Your name is the title of the account. Write your name here.

2. The bank will write in each place that has a circled number 2. Do not write in any of these places.

3. Write the amount of money you want your first deposit to be.

4. You are the primary party. Write your full address.

5. Write your phone number, including the area code.

6. The left side of this section of the application is for information about the primary party, who is you. Write the information requested. Write your date of birth all in numbers. For example, if you were born on July 9, 1955, you would write "7/9/55." Then write your mother's full name, your father's full name, your spouse's full name, and your social security number.

Front of savings account signature card.

SAVINGS ACCOUNT SIGNATURE CARD

① TITLE
② ACCT NUMBER | ACCT–TYPE CODE ② | DT OPND ② | AMT OPENED ③
④ PRIMARY PARTY ADDRESS
② OCCUP CODE | TELEPHONE NUMBER ⑤ | MALE ☐ FEMALE ☐ | OPND BY ②
⑥ | DT OF BIRTH / MOTHER'S NAME / FATHER'S NAME / SPOUSE'S NAME / SOCIAL SECURITY NO. | ⑦
⑦ SECOND PARTY ADDRESS
ZIP CODE

7. Each of the items with a circled number 7 requires the same information about the person with whom you are sharing the account. Do not write anything in these places.

BACK OF SAVINGS ACCOUNT SIGNATURE CARD

8. Sign the card.
9. Write the year you were born all in numbers.
10. On this line, the person sharing the account with you would write his or her signature and year of birth.
11. Write your company name and address.
12. Write your business telephone number, including the area code.
13. If you are sharing the account with someone, write how you are related to this person. For example, you could write "mother/daughter," "husband/wife," or any other relationship.
14. The bank will fill in this section. Do not write anything here.

26 CHAPTER 2 BANK FORMS

Back of savings account signature card.

AGREEMENT

I/WE agree to all of the terms and conditions contained in the by-laws, rules and regulations of THE FIRST CITY BANK FOR SAVINGS, ("the Bank"), as well as all amendments thereof, and to all of the following conditions. IF THIS IS A JOINT ACCOUNT, it is agreed that the balance on deposit may be paid to either during our lifetimes, and on the death of either, to the survivor. Each of us authorizes the other (1) to deposit in the account monies of the other, and to endorse the name of either on any checks, drafts, or any other type of commercial paper, which is payable or endorsed to either or both of us, and (2) to borrow sums of money using the balance on deposit in the account as collateral for such loan(s), and on the failure to repay such loan(s), authorizing the withdrawal by the Bank from the account of the sum(s) necessary to repay such loan(s).

⑧ PRIMARY SIGNAT.		YR. OF BIRTH	⑨
⑩ SECOND SIGNAT.		YR. OF BIRTH	
⑪ BUSINESS ADDRESS		BUSINESS TEL. NO.	⑫
⑬ RELATIONSHIP OF PARTIES	ID		⑭

Fill Out the Application

Assume that you are opening the account for yourself only and use your own personal information to fill out the application. You are planning to deposit $50 to open the account.

LESSON 6 APPLICATION FOR SAVINGS ACCOUNT

LESSON 7

Application for Checking Account

Once you are earning steady money, it is a good idea to open a **checking account**. A checking account makes it possible for you to pay your bills, such as your rent or house payments or gas and electric, without having to go to a bank or the post office to get money orders or without having to take cash to different places. A checking account also provides you with a place to keep your money so that you do not have to carry a lot of cash with you.

Different banks offer different benefits with checking accounts. Some banks give you interest for the money you keep in your checking account. This is usually not as high as the interest in savings accounts, but your money will still earn some money. Banks usually charge you for the service they provide in handling your checks. This is a **service fee**. Some banks charge a certain amount for each check that you write plus a monthly fee for the checking account. Other banks do not charge a monthly fee but may charge for each check.

You should shop around for the bank that offers the most for your money, just as you would for a new car or stereo.

▶ *Be Prepared*

As with the application for a savings account (in Lesson 6), you will fill out a signature card as the application for your checking account. Your signature will be on file with the bank. When you want to withdraw money, the teller will match the signature you write with the signature on file to make sure that your money is being given to the right person.

Only basic information is needed on the signature card. However, you will be asked for your mother's maiden name. If you do not know it, be sure to find it out before you go to the bank.

You will also be asked about the kind of checking account you want. With a **regular checking account**, you must keep a minimum balance or you will be charged a fee. This means that you always have to have a certain amount of money in the account. The amount required is often several thousand dollars. If your balance goes below the minimum amount, you will be charged a fee.

With a **special checking account**, you do not have to keep a minimum balance. Also, you may not be charged a monthly fee. This may depend on the number of transactions you have a month. **Transactions** are the number of checks you write plus the number of deposits and withdrawals you make. If you do not think that you will write many checks or make many deposits or withdrawals, this might be the kind of account for you.

When you open your account with the bank, you will meet with a bank officer. If you have any questions or are not sure about something, ask the bank officer. It is the officer's job to help you, and many people have questions about banking.

Application for Checking Account Vocabulary

amendment   A change.

joint account   An account that is shared by two or more people.

maiden name   A woman's last name before she was married.

statement   A record of the monthly activities of a bank account, such as checks written and deposits made.

How to Fill Out the Application

The following hints will help you fill out the application. The numbers in the following list match the circled numbers on the application. Some parts of the application do not have circled numbers. You should be able to fill in these parts of the application without any special hints or explanation.

FRONT OF THE APPLICATION FOR CHECKING ACCOUNT

1. Check the box for regular checking if that is the kind of account you want. If you want special checking, check that box. If you are not sure, leave this part of the form blank. You can fill it in after you have met with the bank officer.

2. If the checking account is for you only, check the Individual box. If you are going to have the account with someone else, check the Joint box, which stands for **joint account**.

3. Your account number will be assigned to you by the bank officer. Do not write anything here.

4. Write your name in the order noted—your last name first and then your first name.

5. Write your birth date all in numbers. For example, if your birth date is May 18, 1969, write "5/18/69."

6. Write your home telephone number, including the area code.

7. Write your work telephone number, including the area code.

PERSONAL CHECKING ACCOUNT SIGNATURE CARD

1 ☐ Regular Checking *2* ☐ Individual   Account Number   *3*
   ☐ Special Checking   ☐ Joint

4 Print/Type Last Name First | Print/Type Last Name First

Signature | Signature

Home Address (Include Zip) | Home Address (Include Zip)

Social Security Number | *5* Date of Birth | Social Security Number | Date of Birth

6 Home Telephone | *7* Business Telephone | Home Telephone | Business Telephone   *8*

Name and Address of Employer (Include Zip) | Name and Address of Employer (Include Zip)

Citizen of (Country) | Citizen of (Country)

Mother's Maiden Name | Mother's Maiden Name

---

8. If you were opening a joint account, the person sharing the account with you would fill in this side of the card. You should not write anything on this side.

BACK OF THE APPLICATION FOR CHECKING ACCOUNT

9. The bank officer will fill in these two lines. Do not write anything here.

10. Every month, the bank will send you a statement. This is a record of the checks you wrote and deposits you made for the month. If you want the statement to be sent to your home address, check the Home box. If you want the statement to be sent to your work address, check the Business box. If you want it sent to some other address, check the Other box. Then on the line after the word *Specify*, write where you want the statement sent.

11. You will have to pay for the monthly fee and the charge for each check. Most people want these charges automatically subtracted from their accounts. If this is what you want, check the Charge box. If you want a bill for these charges to be mailed to you separately, check the No Charge box.

(9)
Name and Address of Bank References and Account Number

Other Services/Accounts at this Bank

(10)
Send Statement to:
- [ ] Home   [ ] Business   [ ] Other (Specify) _____

(11)
[ ] Charge   [ ] No Charge

I/we (the "Depositor") hereby request the bank to open and maintain an account (the "Account") with the title as indicated on the reverse side of this card which will not be used primarily for a business purpose.

By signing this card, the Depositor agrees that the operation of this Account shall be governed by (a) usual and customary banking practices, (b) local, state or federal laws or regulations (including various estate, inheritance or transfer tax laws, and (c) the "Agreement or Terms and Conditions of Deposit" (and any amendments from time to time) receipt of a signed copy which the Depositor acknowledges.

Signatures

(12) _____

(13) _____

(14) Automatic Payments/Transfers
- [ ] Savings/Bankers Passbook
- [ ] No Charge Checking
- [ ] Direct Deposit (ACH) Program
- [ ] Installment Loan
- [ ] Automatic Transfer of Funds (ATF)
- [ ] Other _____ (Specify)

Interviewer	Signature Verification Accepted By
Reference Verified By	Date Acct. Opened
Introduced By	Date Account Closed
Initial Deposit and Description	
Affiliations	

Back of application for checking account.

12. Sign your name here.

13. If you were opening a joint account, the person sharing the account with you would sign his or her name on this line.

14. The bank officer will fill in everything in this section. Do not write anything here.

Fill Out the Application

Use your own personal information to fill out the form as if you were opening an individual, special checking account.

LESSON 8

Bank Deposit

When you have a savings or checking account and you want to put money into the account, you must fill out a deposit slip. A **deposit slip** provides the bank with a record of the amount you are putting into your account. You are given a copy of the deposit slip, so that you can have a record also.

Some banks have deposit slips that are to be used only for savings accounts. For savings accounts, some banks provide a **passbook**, which is a small book in which your name and account number are printed. Each time you deposit or withdraw money, you give the passbook to the bank teller. The teller makes a record in the passbook of the amount put in or taken out. A record of the interest you have earned will also be made.

Other banks do not provide a passbook for a savings account. Instead, you are given a small book in which you keep your own record of deposits and withdrawals. Once a month, you will receive a statement from the bank that shows all the deposits and withdrawals for the month. This statement also tells you how much interest your money has earned.

Some banks have deposit slips that are to be used only for checking accounts. Often, you get a supply of deposit slips for checking accounts when you open the account. Your name and account number are printed on the deposit slips.

Sometimes, banks have one deposit slip that can be used for either savings or checking accounts. That is the type of deposit slip shown in this book.

▸ Be Prepared

Deposit slips are small forms, and they are easy to fill out. You do not have to provide a lot of information. You will need to know your account number and the exact amount you are depositing.

▸ How to Fill Out the Bank Deposit

The following hints will help you fill out the deposit slip. The numbers in the following list match the circled numbers on the form. Some parts of the form do not have circled numbers. You should be able to fill in these parts of the form without any special hints or explanation.

1. Write the date in words and numbers. It is OK to abbreviate the month. For example, January could be written as "Jan.," February as "Feb.," and so on.

2. Write your name the same way it appears on your account. That is, write your name the way you wrote it when you filled out the application for your savings or checking account.

3. If you are making a deposit into your checking account, check the Checking box. If you are making a deposit into your savings account, check the Savings box.

4. Write your account number. Each number of the account number should be written in each of the boxes.

5. If you are depositing cash, write the total amount of cash you are depositing.

6. If you are depositing checks, write the amount of each check on a separate line. For example, if you had two checks, one for $50 and one for $73, you would write "50.00" on the first line of circled item 6 and "73.00" on the next line.

7. Add up the amount of the cash and checks you are depositing and write the total here. If you are depositing only one check or only cash, this total will be the same as the amount above.

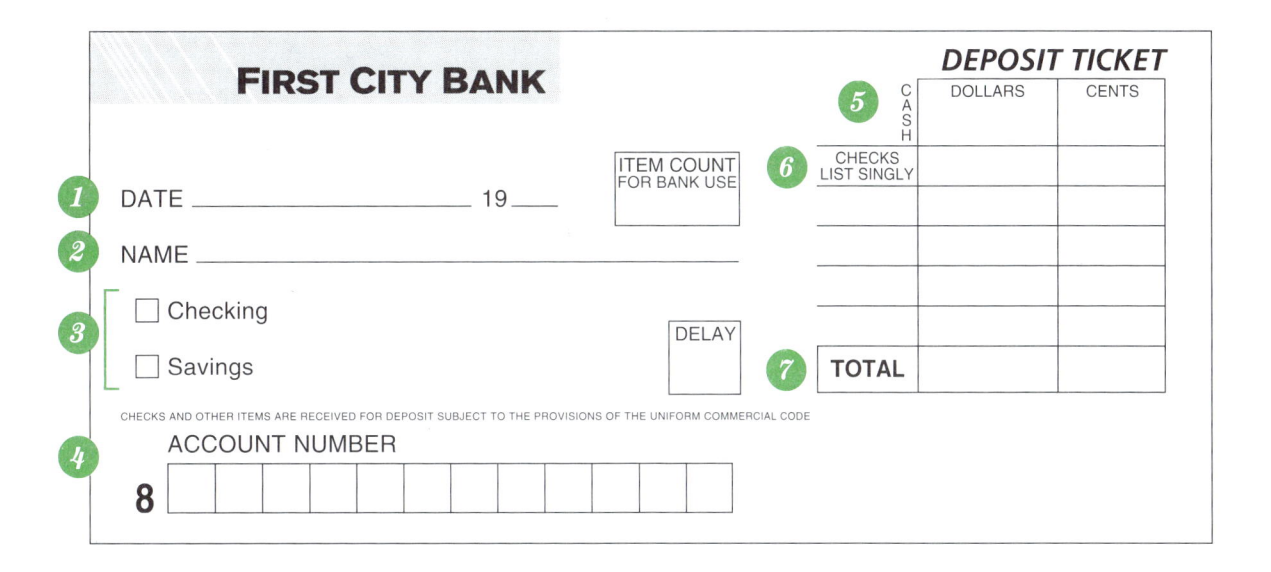

Fill Out the Bank Deposit

Use today's date and your name. Fill out the deposit slip, using the following information:

- You want to make a deposit to your checking account.
- Your account number is 037245936784.
- You are depositing $54 in cash and three checks for the following amounts: $125.87, $258.09, and $62.00.

LESSON 8   BANK DEPOSIT   **33**

LESSON 9

Withdrawal from Savings

Once you open a checking or savings account, you will probably keep most of your money in the bank. Of course, you need cash to pay for your living expenses, such as food, transportation, and housing. You can get cash from your checking account by writing a check to yourself or to "Cash" (see how to do this in Lesson 11). If you want to get cash from your savings account, you must fill out a form called a **withdrawal slip**.

Many people use automated teller machines (ATMs) to get cash. ATMs are computerized machines that let people take care of banking activities without going into the bank. These machines are usually located right outside a bank. Sometimes, they are in the lobby of a bank. One advantage of an ATM is that you can do your banking during hours when the bank is closed. Another advantage is that you can do your banking at any bank branch.

In addition to withdrawing money, you can perform other banking activities with ATMs. You can:

- Find out the balance of your account.
- Make a deposit.
- Transfer money from your savings to your checking account or from your checking to your savings account.

If you have a passbook savings account, you cannot use an ATM. Instead, you must go to the bank, fill out a withdrawal slip, and withdraw cash by going to a teller.

▶ *Be Prepared*

In Lesson 6, you filled out an application for a savings account. The application was in the form of a signature card. Your bank keeps your signature card on file. When you want to withdraw money from your account, you must sign a withdrawal slip. The bank teller will then check to see that the signature on the withdrawal slip matches the signature on file. No one can withdraw money from your account without your signature.

A withdrawal slip is a short, simple form. You must have your account number in order to fill it out. If you have a passbook savings account, you must also bring your passbook when you go to the bank so that the teller can make a record in the passbook of the amount of money you have withdrawn.

How to Fill Out the Withdrawal Slip

The following hints will help you fill out the withdrawal slip. The numbers in the following list match the circled numbers on the slip. Some parts of the slip do not have circled numbers. You should be able to fill in these parts of the slip without any special hints or explanation.

1. Write the date in words and numbers or all in numbers. For example, you can write the date as "April 3, 1993," or as "4/3/93."

2. Write the amount of money you want to withdraw all in words. Here are a few things to remember when you write amounts of money all in words.

   a. For amounts over $1,000, such as $1,233, write thousands, then hundreds, then tens, and then ones. For example, $1,233 would be written as "One thousand two hundred thirty-three," not "Twelve hundred thirty-three."

   b. Remember to hyphenate numbers such as 24 (twenty-four) or 57 (fifty-seven).

   c. Do not put an "and" between the hundreds and the tens. For example, 649 would be written as "Six hundred forty-nine," not "Six hundred and forty-nine."

   d. To write cents, first write "and" after the last dollar amount. Then write the cents as a fraction, with the number of cents over 100. For example, $289.51 would be written as "Two hundred eighty-nine and $\frac{51}{100}$." You must do this even if you do not want any cents. If there are no cents in the amount, you should write "$\frac{00}{100}$."

3. Write the amount in numbers. The dollar amount should go to the left of the tick mark. The cents should go to the right of the tick mark. If there are no cents, write two zeros.

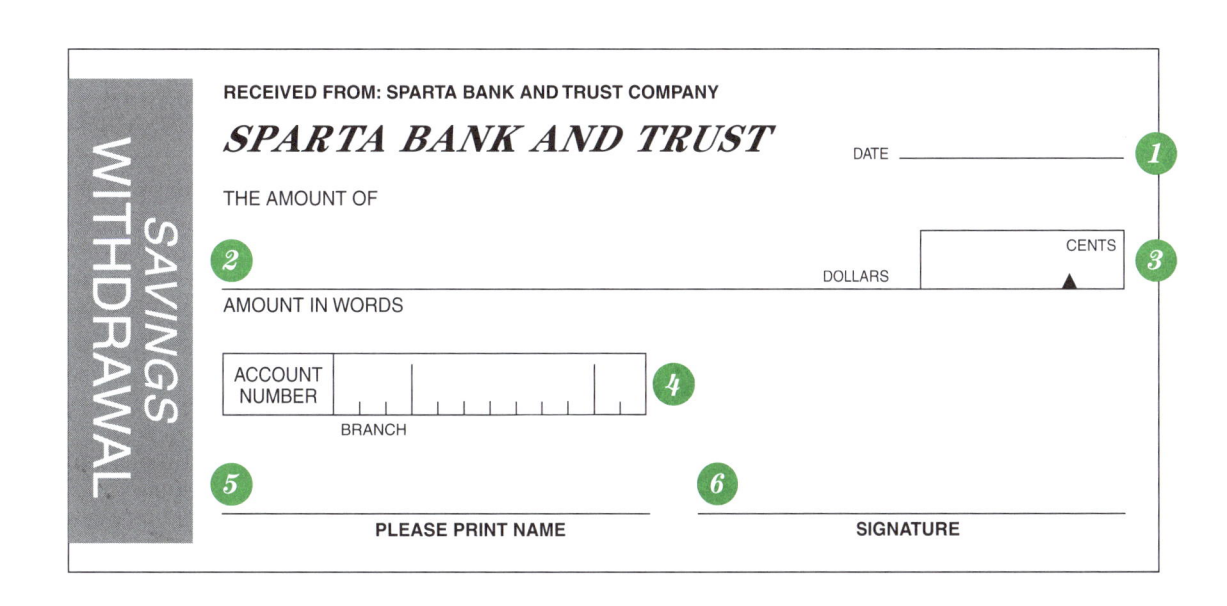

LESSON 9 WITHDRAWAL FROM SAVINGS **35**

4. Write your account number by placing each number of your account number between the tick marks.

5. Print your name as it appears on your account.

6. Write your signature as it appears on your account.

Fill Out the Withdrawal Slip

Fill out the withdrawal slip using today's date and your own name. You want to withdraw $368.02. Your account number is 213-4466579-47.

LESSON 10

Checks and Check Register

Once you open a checking account, you can use your checks to pay your bills. The following information will be on your checks:

- Your name and address
- Preprinted check numbers
- The name and address of your bank
- Your checking account number

Checks come in different colors. Some checks have pictures on them. When you open your account, the bank officer will show you the kinds of checks available, and you can pick the ones you like. You will also be asked to pick a checkbook, which is a protective folder in which your checks fit.

You will also have to decide what type of check records you want to keep. Every time you write a check or make a deposit to your checking account, you must write down exactly what you have done so that you can keep track of how much money you have. In some cases, you can keep your record on a check stub. The stub is connected to the check with a perforation. Whenever you write a check, you fill in the stub. Then, when you remove the check from the checkbook, the stub remains as a record of the amount of the check you have written.

Stubs may be connected to checks at the side (as shown below) or at the top (as shown at the top of the next page).

Check with side stub.

LESSON 10 CHECKS AND CHECK REGISTER 37

BAL.	830	92
DEPOSIT		
TOTAL	830	92
THIS ITEM	42	25
OTHER DED. (IF ANY)		
BAL.	788	67

1280

DATE April 5, 19 — $ 42 25/100
TO Dade Telephone
FOR (305) 555-9870 phone bill

Your Name
6390 Collins Avenue
Miami Beach, FL 33141

1280

64-5387 / 610

April 5, 19 —

Pay to the Order of Dade Telephone $ 42 25/100

Fourty-two and 25/100 ——————————— Dollars

MIAMI BANK
Miami, Florida 33162

FOR (305) 555-9870 — phone bill

⑈0610⑆5387⑈

Check with top stub.

Many people prefer to have a check register rather than a stub. A check register is made up of pages that are usually placed at the front of your checkbook. Every time you write a check, you must remember to fill out the check register. You also record deposits in the check register. Checks with a check register are the kind used in this book.

CHECK NO.	DATE	CHECK ISSUED TO	AMOUNT OF CHECK	✓	DATE OF DEP.	AMOUNT OF DEPOSIT	BALANCE	
							830	92
1280	4/5	Dade Telephone	42.25				788	67
					4/7	390.22	1,178	89

Check register.

▶ Be Prepared

Filling out a check is like filling out a withdrawal slip (Lesson 9) or a money order (Lesson 18). Much of the information you would usually write on many forms is already printed on the check (your name, the check number, and your checking account number). So there is not much for you to write.

If you are using a check to pay a bill, you should go over the bill to be sure you have the information you need:

- The name the check should be made out to.
- The exact amount to write the check for.
- The account number printed on the bill. For each of the companies that send you bills, you have an account number. For example, you have account numbers with your electric or phone company, with your credit card department store or bank, and with your cable TV company. You should write the account numbers on the checks in the space provided.

Once you have gone over the bill, you are ready to write the check.

Check and Check Register Vocabulary

balance The amount in a bank account.

issued to Written or directed to.

▶ How to Fill Out a Check and a Check Register

The following hints will help you fill out a check and a check register. The numbers in the following lists match the circled numbers on the check and check register. Some parts do not have circled numbers. You should be able to fill in these parts of the check and check register without any special hints or explanation.

CHECK

1. Write the date in words and numbers. Put the last two numbers of the year after the *19* printed on the check.

2. Write the name of the person or company you are writing the check to. Be sure to begin writing at the very left of the printed line, next to the words *Order of*. After you write the name, draw a line from the end of the name to the dollar sign. By starting to write at the very left and drawing a line, you make it hard for someone to change or add to what you have written. (Look at the check shown with a stub earlier in this lesson.)

```
                                                                    0701
      Your Name
      1711 Main Street
      Atlanta, GA 30310
                                                                    64-5387
                                                                    ─────
                                                                     610
                              ①  _____ 19 ____
  ②  Pay to the
      Order of _____ $ _____   ③

  ④  _____ Dollars

      [Bank of GEORGIA]  309 PEACHTREE DRIVE
                         ATLANTA, GA  30303

  ⑤  FOR _____         _____   ⑥
      ⑆0610⑆ 5387⑈ 398 ⑈ 7241⑈
```

3. Write the amount of the check all in numbers. Write the cents as a fraction, with the number of cents over 100. For example, $45.98 should be written as "$45 \frac{98}{100}$."

4. Write the amount of the check all in words beginning at the very left edge of the line. Here are a few things to remember when you write amounts of money all in words.

   a. For amounts over $1,000, such as $1,233, write thousands, then hundreds, then tens, and then ones. For example, $1,233 would be written as "One thousand two hundred thirty-three," not "Twelve hundred thirty-three."

   b. Remember to hyphenate numbers such as 24 (twenty-four) or 57 (fifty-seven).

   c. Do not put an "and" between the hundreds and the tens. For example, 649 would be written as "Six hundred forty-nine," not "Six hundred and forty-nine."

   d. To write cents, first write "and" after the last dollar amount and then write the cents as a fraction, with the number of cents over 100. For example, $289.51 would be written as "Two hundred eighty-nine and $\frac{51}{100}$." You must do this even if you do not want any cents. If there are no cents in the amount, you should write "$\frac{00}{100}$."

   After you have written the amount, draw a line from the cents fraction to the word *Dollars*. By starting at the left and drawing the line, you prevent someone from changing the amount you have written. (Look at the check shown with a stub earlier in the lesson.)

5. If you are paying a bill, write your account number here. You may also use this line to make a note. For example, if you owe someone money and are writing a check to pay the debt, you can write something like, "Loan, paid in full."

6. Sign your name as it appears on the account.

CHECK NO.	DATE	CHECK ISSUED TO	AMOUNT OF CHECK	✓	DATE OF DEP.	AMOUNT OF DEPOSIT	BALANCE
							927 83

CHECK REGISTER

If you are recording that you wrote a check, refer to items 7, 8, 9, 10, 11, 12, and 15. If you are recording that you made a deposit, refer to items 7, 13, 14, and 15.

7. Write the amount that you have in your checking account. This may be the starting balance or the balance carried over from the preceding page of the register. Use the wider, left-hand column for dollars and the narrower, right-hand column for cents. The balance has been written on the check register shown here. (If you are making a deposit, go to item 13.)

8. Write the check number.

9. Write the month and the day all in numbers. For example, write January 23 as "1/23." (There is no room to write the year.)

10. Write the name of the person or company you wrote the check to.

11. Write the amount of the check.

12. You will use this column when you check your check register against the records the bank sends you. Do not write anything here now. (Items 13 and 14 are for deposits only. If you are writing a check, go to item 15.)

13. Write the month and the day of the deposit all in numbers. (See item 9 above for how to do this.)

14. Write the amount of the deposit.

15. If you wrote a check, *subtract* the amount of the check from the balance shown directly above the line on which you recorded the check. If you made a deposit, *add* the amount of the deposit to the balance shown directly above the line on which you recorded the deposit. Write the new balance on the line on

LESSON 10 CHECKS AND CHECK REGISTER   **41**

which you recorded the check or the deposit. This way, you will always know exactly how much money you have in your checking account. (Look at the check register shown earlier in this lesson.)

Write Checks and Fill Out the Check Register

You want to pay some bills by check. Use the following information to fill out the checks and the check register. Use today's date and your own name. Use the check register shown earlier in this lesson, and then use the three checks on page 43.

Check to: Ideal Cable Company

Amount: $34.97

Account number: 1424-3798-21

Check to: Barkley Realty

Amount: $623.45

Account number: 38-654-01-4

You want to make a deposit in the amount of $326.88. Record the deposit in the check register.

You need some cash for the weekend. Write a check to yourself (put your name after *Pay to the Order of*) for $150. Or write a check to "Cash" (write the word "Cash" after *Pay to the Order of*) for $150. Record the check in the check register.

Your Name	0701
1711 Main Street	
Atlanta, GA 30310	64-5387 / 610

_____ 19____

Pay to the
Order of _____ $ _____

_____ Dollars

Bank of GEORGIA 309 PEACHTREE DRIVE
ATLANTA, GA 30303

FOR _____

⑈0610⑈ 5387⑈ 398 ⑈ 7241⑈

Your Name	0702
1711 Main Street	
Atlanta, GA 30310	64-5387 / 610

_____ 19____

Pay to the
Order of _____ $ _____

_____ Dollars

Bank of GEORGIA 309 PEACHTREE DRIVE
ATLANTA, GA 30303

FOR _____

⑈0610⑈ 5387⑈ 398 ⑈ 7241⑈

Your Name	0703
1711 Main Street	
Atlanta, GA 30310	64-5387 / 610

_____ 19____

Pay to the
Order of _____ $ _____

_____ Dollars

Bank of GEORGIA 309 PEACHTREE DRIVE
ATLANTA, GA 30303

FOR _____

⑈0610⑈ 5387⑈ 398 ⑈ 7241⑈

LESSON 11

Check Endorsement

Most companies pay their employees by check. You may also receive a check as a gift or for some other reason. You cannot cash a check, deposit it in your savings or checking account, or give it to someone else until you endorse it. Although endorsing a check is not quite the same as filling out a form, it is an important part of banking and is something you should know about.

When you **endorse a check**, you sign it on the back. There are a few different ways that checks can be endorsed. With the first way, you write just your signature on the back of the check. When you endorse a check this way, it can be cashed by anyone. For this reason, you should not endorse a check in this way unless you are at the bank and ready to cash or deposit the check.

With the second kind of endorsement, you sign your name and you *also* say how the check is to be used. Most often, this means that you will write "For deposit only," which means that the check cannot be used for anything except a deposit.

Sometimes, you may want to give the check to someone else. Because the check is made out to you, no one else can cash it unless you endorse the check over to another person. To do this, you sign your name, write the words "Pay to the Order of," and then write the name of the person to whom you are giving the check.

If you have a checking or savings account at the bank at which you are cashing or depositing a check, you should always write your bank account number on the back of the check. If you write only your signature as the endorsement, put the account number under your

② Orrin Jackson
③ 0140772323-15

signature. If you are going to deposit the check, put the account number under the words "For deposit only."

▸ Be Prepared

Because endorsing a check is not quite the same as filling out a form, there is little or no preparation necessary. If you have an account at the bank where you are cashing or depositing the check, you should write your account number as part of the endorsement.

▸ How to Endorse a Check

1. First hold the check face up in front of you. The left side of the front of the check is the top of the check when you turn it over to endorse it.

2. No matter what type of endorsement you decide to use, always write your signature at the top as the first item.

3. If you endorse the check by writing only your signature, and you have a bank account at the bank where you are cashing the check, write your bank account number below your signature (look at the endorsement on page 44).

4. If you want to deposit the check, write "For deposit only." Then write your bank account number (see the endorsement below at the left).

5. If you want to endorse the check to someone else, write "Pay to the order of" and then the name of the person to whom you are endorsing the check (see the endorsement below at the right).

② *Marlene Wooden*
④ *For deposit only*
   973-2970-1118-1

② *Nora O'Connor*
⑤ *Pay to the order of*
   Jason Bowman

LESSON 11 CHECK ENDORSEMENT **45**

Endorse Checks

Read the following information and then decide how each check should be endorsed. Write the correct endorsement on the backs of the checks provided at the end of the lesson.

1. Your aunt gives you a $25 check as a gift. You meet with a friend whom you owe $25. Rather than giving your friend cash, you decide to give your friend the check your aunt gave you.

2. You receive your paycheck, and you want to deposit the whole check in your savings account. Your account number is 01-3768992.

3. You did some work for a neighbor, who pays you by check. You want to cash the check at the bank where you have your checking account. Your account number is 32-324533-33.

46 CHAPTER 2 BANK FORMS

LESSON 12

Bank Statement Reconciliation

When you have a checking account, the bank will send you a bank statement every month. The statement is the bank's record of all the checks you wrote and all the deposits you made during the month. It is important that you compare your records with the bank's records to make sure they agree.

On the back of the bank statement is a form—the **bank statement reconciliation form**—that you should use to check your records against the bank's records. The word **reconcile** means "to make things agree." The word **reconciliation** means an "agreement" between two or more things.

When you write a check to pay your telephone bill, for example, the check is received by the phone company. The phone company sends your check to its bank. The phone company's bank deposits your check so that the phone company can receive its payment, just the way you do when you get your paycheck. Then the phone company's bank sends your check to your bank for payment. Your bank takes the money from your checking account to pay for the amount you wrote on the check. The money is then deducted from your account. When this happens, your check has cleared the bank. This means that your check has been processed and the amount written on the check has been paid.

The amount of time it takes for a check to clear varies, depending on:
- When the people or companies you wrote the check to bring your check to their bank
- How long it takes for their bank to get the check to your bank
- How long it takes for your bank to pay the amount of the check

The dates on the bank statement are the dates the checks you wrote cleared your bank. The order of the checks on the statement is the order in which your checks cleared, starting with the one that cleared first. This order will often be different from the order in which you wrote the checks.

Included with the bank statement will be the actual checks that you wrote. These checks are called **canceled checks**. They have been endorsed on the back by the people or companies you wrote them to. They also have the amount of the check printed on the bottom right part of the front of the check. This is how you can tell that a check has been canceled. The canceled checks are arranged in the order in which they cleared the bank, not the order in which you wrote them. The check amounts printed on the statement are in the same order as the canceled checks.

The bank statement also shows a record of the deposits you made during the month. The dates for the deposits will be the same as the dates you made them, since deposits do not have to travel from one bank to another.

Some banks charge a monthly fee for the banking service they provide. Some also charge you a certain amount of money for each check that you write. This varies from one bank to another. On the bank statement the service charges appear as an amount that is subtracted from the total. You must remember to subtract this amount from your own bank records before you begin to reconcile your records with the bank statement.

▶ *Be Prepared*

In order for you to do the bank statement reconciliation, you will need your records of all the banking you did for the month. These records will appear on your check register or your check stubs. (See Lesson 10 for information about check registers and check stubs.)

It is a good idea to have a calculator to help you with the arithmetic you must do to reconcile your records with the bank statement. If you do not have a calculator, you can buy a small pocket calculator for around $10. If you do not want to use a calculator, you can do the arithmetic yourself.

Bank Statement Reconciliation Vocabulary

balance The amount of money in a bank account.

closing date The last day of the month covered by the bank statement. All checks written and all deposits made after the closing date will appear on the next month's statement.

credit An amount added to a bank account.

debit An amount subtracted from a bank account.

outstanding check A check that has been written but does not appear on the bank statement.

▶ *How to Do a Bank Statement Reconciliation*

Before you begin working on the bank statement reconciliation, make sure that your check register is up to date. If you have not figured the balance for the last check you wrote or deposit you made, do this now. Also, look over the bank statement to see whether there are any bank or service charges. If there are, subtract the amount of these charges from the balance in your check register. In addition, enter today's date in the *Date* column and write "Bank service charges" or something similar in the *Check Issued To* column.

STATEMENT

1. Put the canceled checks in order by check number. Place the check with the lowest number first.

2. Keep the checks and the front of the bank statement handy. Turn to your check register (or check stubs).

3. Refer to the first canceled check in the group of checks. Compare the amount of this check against the amounts on the bank statement in the *Checks & Other Debits* column. If the amount of the check appears on the statement, place a check mark next to the amount on the statement.

4. Then find the record of this check that you made in the check register. Put a check mark in the column that has a check mark at the top.

5. Do the same for all the canceled checks.

6. Now look at the *Deposits & Other Credits* column of the bank statement. Compare the amounts shown here with the amounts on your check register.

BANK OF MINNEAPOLIS
309 MAIN STREET
MINNEAPOLIS, MN 55420

STATEMENT OF ACCOUNT NUMBER
398 7241

Your Name
1711 Main Street
Minneapolis, MN 55421

CLOSING DATE
3/26/-

CHECKING ACCOUNT STATEMENT

BEGINNING BALANCE	(+) TOTAL CREDITS	(−) TOTAL DEBITS	(−) SERVICE CHARGE	(=) NEW BALANCE
722.98	893.96	927.78	1.50	689.16

CHECKS & OTHER DEBITS		DEPOSITS & OTHER CREDITS	DATE	BALANCE
		446.98	3/4	1169.96
573.48			3/5	596.48
29.87			3/7	566.61
75.00	37.93		3/9	453.68
150.00			3/13	303.68
		446.98	3/19	750.66
60.00			3/20	690.66
1.50 SC			3/26	689.16

Bank statement.

7. When you find a deposit on the statement that is the same amount as a deposit in your check register, put a check mark next to the amount in the check register. Do this for all deposits. You are now ready to reconcile the bank statement with your check register.

RECONCILIATION

The following hints will help you fill out the reconciliation form. The numbers in the following list match the circled numbers on the form.

1. The amount you should write here is on the statement. You can find it either in the *New Balance* box at the top or at the bottom of the *Balance* column. Write the dollar amount in the wider column, and write the cents in the narrower column.

2. Look through your check register and find the deposits that do not appear on the bank statement. If more than one deposit is missing, add up all the deposits that do not appear on the statement and write the total here.

3. Add the amount that you wrote in item 1 to the amount that you wrote in item 2. Write the total of these numbers.

④ OUTSTANDING CHECKS

NUMBER	AMOUNT
⑤ TOTAL	

Reconciliation form.

TO RECONCILE YOUR STATEMENT AND CHECKBOOK

1. DEDUCT FROM YOUR CHECKBOOK BALANCE ANY SERVICE OR OTHER CHARGE MADE BY THE BANK. THESE CHARGES ARE LABELED SC.

2. ARRANGE ENDORSED CHECKS BY DATE OR NUMBER AND CHECK THEM OFF AGAINST THE RECORDS IN YOUR CHECKBOOK.

3. LIST IN THE OUTSTANDING CHECKS SECTION AT THE LEFT ANY CHECKS ISSUED BY YOU AND NOT YET PAID BY US.

TO RECONCILE YOUR STATEMENT AND CHECKBOOK

LAST BALANCE SHOWN ON STATEMENT		①
PLUS: Deposits and Credits Made After Date of Last Entry on Statement		②
SUBTOTAL		③
MINUS: Outstanding Checks		⑥
BALANCE: Which Should Agree with Your Checkbook		⑦

50 CHAPTER 2 BANK FORMS

4. Look through your check register and find all the checks that you wrote but that do not appear on the bank statement (the outstanding checks). Start with the check with the lowest number. Write the check number in the *Number* column, and write the amount of the check in the *Amount* column. Write the dollar amount in the wider column, and write the cents in the narrower column.

5. After you have written all the outstanding checks, add them up and write the total.

6. Write the total of the outstanding checks (item 5).

7. Subtract the total of the outstanding checks (item 6) from the subtotal (item 3). This amount should be the same as the balance in your check register.

If the balance on the reconciliation form and the balance in your check register are not the same, first make sure that you remembered to subtract the service charge. If the two balances are still not the same, double-check all the math you did on the reconciliation form. If the balances still do not match, double-check all your math in your check register.

If you try all this and you still find that the balances do not match, check the canceled checks against the amount of the checks you wrote in the register. These should be the same. If you try all these things, you should be able to find the error.

Do a Bank Statement Reconciliation

Once a month, you receive your bank statement (shown on page 49) and canceled checks in the mail. A list of the canceled checks is shown here. The checks are listed in check number order. Your check register for the month is shown on page 52.

CANCELED CHECKS

CHECK NO.	DATE WRITTEN	FOR	AMOUNT
206	2/27	Rent	$ 573.48
207	3/2	Telephone	29.87
208	3/4	Gas and electric	37.93
209	3/4	Department store credit card	75.00
210	3/11	Cash	150.00
211	3/14	Bank credit card	60.00

Before you begin to reconcile the bank statement with your check register, look over the statement to see whether there are any bank or service charges. If there are, subtract these charges from your balance. Now compare the canceled checks, the check register, and the bank statement. Next compare the deposits in the check register against the deposits shown on the statement. Then use the reconciliation form (on page 50), the check information (on page 51), and the check register (below) to do the bank statement reconciliation. If the balances do not match, double-check all your math.

CHECK NO.	DATE	CHECK ISSUED TO	AMOUNT OF CHECK	✓	DATE OF DEP.	AMOUNT OF DEPOSIT	BALANCE 722	98
206	2/27	Twin City Realty	573.48				149	50
207	3/2	Minneapolis Telephone	29.87				119	63
					3/4	446.98	566	61
208	3/4	Minn. Gas & Electric	37.93				528	68
209	3/4	Milano Dept. Store	75.00				453	68
210	3/11	Cash	150.00				303	68
211	3/14	Master Card	60.00				243	68
212	3/14	Minnco Cable	25.00				218	68
					3/18	446.98	665	66
213	3/24	Bus. Mag. renewal	32.40				663	26

LESSON 13

Application for Car Loan

People who want to buy something very expensive, such as a house or a car, often do not have enough money on hand or saved up to buy what they want. So they may borrow money from a bank.

Banks need a lot of information before they will make a loan. This is because they need to know that people who borrow money will be able to repay it.

Also, banks charge interest for the loans they make. The interest is a percentage of the amount that is borrowed.

People pay back loans in installments. This means that you must pay a certain amount every month until the loan is paid off.

When you take out a loan, you should decide how long you will take to pay it back. This will depend on how much the loan is for, how much interest the bank will charge, and how much you can truly afford to pay each month. The bank officer will help you figure out all these things.

▶ Be Prepared

You need to be prepared with a lot of information about your personal finances. The bank will want to know about the following:
- Your salary and other sources of income
- Things you own of value, such as a life insurance policy
- All information about other loans you may have
- The amount of your monthly mortgage or rent payment
- All information about your bank accounts
- If you have a home mortgage, all information about it, such as the amount of the mortgage
- All information about your credit cards

The bank will also want some basic information about your job. And, if you are applying for a car loan, you should know the kind of car and the price of the car you want to buy.

Application for Car Loan Vocabulary

credit line In charge accounts, the maximum amount of money that the holder of the charge account is permitted to charge.

credit outstanding The amount owed.

creditor Person or company to whom money is owed.

dependents People who depend on you for financial support.

disclose   Reveal.

face value   The amount something is worth.

installment   One loan payment; usually paid once a month.

surrender value   The amount something would be worth if it were turned in, or cashed in.

How to Fill Out an Application for a Car Loan

The following hints will help you fill out the application. The numbers in the following list match the circled numbers on the application. Some parts of the application do not have circled numbers. You should be able to fill in these parts of the application without any special hints or explanation.

1. Write the amount of the loan you want. Then check the box indicating how long you will take to repay the loan.

2. Write your birth date all in numbers. For example, if you were born on June 12, 1960, write "6/12/60."

3. Write your social security number so that each number in the social security number fits within the tick marks.

4. Write how long you have lived at your current address. Write the number of years above *Yrs.* and the number of months above *Mos.*

5. Write how many dependents you have.

6. If you own your home, check the first box. If you rent a house or apartment, check the second box.

7. If you own a home, write the amount of your monthly mortgage payments. If you rent, write your monthly rental payments.

8. Write the address of the place where you lived before you moved to where you live now. Write only the house number and street on this line. Write the city, state, and zip code on the next line.

9. Write the name of the company you work for. Write the city, state, and zip code on the next line.

10. Write the amount of money you earn in a whole year *before* taxes and other deductions are taken out.

11. Write in years (*Yrs.*) and months (*Mos.*) how long you have worked at your current job.

12. Include the area code when you write your business telephone number.

CREDIT APPLICATION

$3,000 Minimum Loan, Check Applicable Box(es)

(1) For Auto or Home Improvement Loans
I apply for an installment loan of $ _____   For loan amounts between $3,000 and $4,999 ☐ 24 mos. ☐ 36 mos. ☐ 48 mos.
For loan amounts between $5,000 and $15,000 ☐ 24 mos. ☐ 36 mos. ☐ 48 mos. ☐ 60 mos.

TELL US ABOUT YOURSELF Applicant   PLEASE PRINT AND COMPLETE ALL INFORMATION

☐ Mr. ☐ Ms. ☐ Mrs.   **(2)** Date of Birth Mo. Day Year   **(3)** Social Security Number

Last Name   First Name   Initial   Home Address   Apartment

City   State   Zip   **(4)** How Long Yrs. Mos.   Area Code   Home Tel. No.

(5) No. of Dependents   **(6)** ☐ Own Home ☐ Rent   **(7)** $ _____ Monthly Payment   **(8)** Previous Home Address   How Long Yrs. Mos.

City   State   Zip   **(9)** Name of Business or Employer

Business Address   City   State   Zip   **(10)** Annual Salary   **(11)** How Long Yrs. Mos.   **(12)** Bus. Tel. No.

(13) Type of Business   **(14)** Position

You need not disclose alimony, child support, separate maintenance income or its source, unless you want us to consider it in connection with this application.

(15) $ _____ Other Income   **(16)** Source of Other Income   **(17)** Name of Previous Business or Employer (List only if current employment is less than 3 years)   Position

(18) Business Address   How Long Yrs. Mos.

Total Credit Outstanding other than mortgage $ _____   **(19)** Mo. Pymts. $ _____

CREDIT REFERENCES

Checking Account (Bank Name)   Address   Account Number $

Savings Account (Bank Name)   Address   Account Number   Balance
$ $ $

(20) Home Financed By   Address   Original Mortgage   Estimated Value   Mortgage Balance

LOANS Please list all loans. (Attach separate sheet, if necessary.)

1. $ $ $
Creditor   Address   Account No.   Original Amount   Balance   Monthly Pymt.
2. $ $ $
Creditor   Address   Account No.   Original Amount   Balance   Monthly Pymt.

CREDIT CARDS AND CREDIT LINES

1. $ $ $
Creditor   Address   Account No.   Credit Line   Balance   Monthly Pymt.
2. $ $ $
Creditor   Address   Account No.   Credit Line   Balance   Monthly Pymt.

OTHER ASSETS

(21) Stocks and Bonds $ $ $

(22) Cash Surrender Value of Life Insurance   **(23)** Issuer   **(24)** $ Policy Face Value
Issuer $ Policy Face Value

(25) Other Financial Assets (Describe in Detail) $ $ $

Total Assets   **(26)** $

Do you own a car? ☐ Yes ☐ No   Year and Make _____

(27) **Car Purchase Information** (if this is an auto loan)

Year	Make	Price $	Down Payment $
Seller		To be registered in the name of	
Serial No. if known			

AGREEMENT: By signing below as applicant, I request the credit that I have indicated above. The information I have provided is true and complete. The bank may obtain a consumer credit report(s) from one or more consumer reporting agencies (credit bureaus) in connection with this application and, if credit is granted, reports may also be obtained from time to time in the future. If I request you will inform me whether any consumer credit report was requested and if so, the name and address of the consumer reporting agency or agencies which furnished the report. Also, you may exchange credit information about me in connection with this application and any credit you extend to me.

Please Sign Here
(29) X _____
Applicant's Signature   Date

INCOMPLETE APPLICATIONS WILL NOT BE PROCESSED

(28) Please send mail to my home ☐ office ☐
To reach me quickly, call _____
(Area code) Telephone No. between the hours of _____ and _____ A.M.
P.M.

LESSON 13 APPLICATION FOR CAR LOAN   55

13. Write the kind of business you work for. For example, if you work for a clothing manufacturer, write "Manufacturing."

14. Write your job title.

15. If you have income from something other than the job you listed above, write the amount of money this adds up to for a whole year. If you wish, you may include money you receive as child support or alimony payments.

16. Write where you get the money from.

17. If you have had your present job for less than three years, write the name of the place where you worked before.

18. If you have other loans, write the total amount that you owe.

19. If you have other loans, write the amount of the monthly payments you make.

20. If you have a home mortgage, write the name and address of the bank you received the mortgage from. Then answer the other questions on this line about the mortgage.

21. If you own stocks or bonds, write the kind of stocks or bonds you own and the amount they are worth.

22. If you have one or more life insurance policies, write the amount the policies would be worth if you cashed them in right now.

23. Write the name of the life insurance company.

24. Write the total amount the policy is worth.

25. If you have any other things of value, explain what they are and how much they are worth.

26. Add up how much all the things you listed are worth and write the total here.

27. This section is about the car you plan to buy if the bank gives you the loan.

28. Write the phone number at which you can usually be reached. Then write the time of day that you can be reached.

29. Sign your name and write today's date all in numbers.

Fill Out the Car Loan Application

Use your own personal information to fill out the form. You do not have to check one of the boxes telling how long you will take to repay the loan. You have been saving your money and shopping for a used car. You have found one that you would like to buy from a used-car dealer. The car is a 1990 Mercury Sable LS and costs $7,495. You plan on making a down payment of $3,000 which you have in your savings. The company selling the car is DiNapoli Ford Mercury Used Cars.

CHAPTER 3

MEDICAL FORMS

▲

When you go to a doctor for the first time, you will most likely be asked to fill out a form called a **medical history**. This form gives the doctor important information about your medical background. This information can help the doctor decide on the best way to treat you.

Doctor visits, medical tests, prescriptions for medications, hospital stays, and emergency treatment can cost a lot of money—more than many people can afford to pay on their own. There are ways people can receive help to pay for medical expenses.

With one way, the government pays for a person's medical expenses through medicaid or medicare. With the other way, insurance companies provide health insurance.

LESSON 14

Medical History

When you go to see a doctor for the first time, you will probably be asked to fill out a form that gives the doctor information about your medical background. This helps the doctor to know as much as possible about your medical history so that information about your past can be used to help treat you now.

▸ *Be Prepared*

You will need to know about any medical conditions you had in the past, even when you were a child. If you are not sure about any medical conditions you had as a child, you should find out before you go to the doctor.

If you work for a company that gives you health insurance or if you have an individual health insurance policy, you should know the name of the insurance company and your policy number. If you do not know the policy number, check with your employer's personnel department or with the insurance company.

You should fill out your sections of the medical insurance claim form (Lesson 16) and take the form with you when you go to the doctor.

Medical History Vocabulary

A medical history form lists the names of many diseases and medical conditions. Some of them, such as high blood pressure, are fairly common, and some are less common.

It is difficult to explain medical terms and diseases in a few words. Also, definitions of these terms may not help make it clear to you what they mean. If you are not sure whether you have had any of the diseases or conditions listed on the form, ask the doctor's assistant to explain the terms to you when you are at the doctor's office.

▸ *How to Fill Out a Medical History*

The following hints will help you fill out the medical history. The numbers in the following list match the circled numbers on the form. Some parts of the form do not have circled numbers. You should be able to fill in these parts of the form without any special hints or explanation.

1. Write today's date all in numbers. For example, if today is March 24, 1994, write "3/24/94."

2. Write your date of birth all in numbers.
3. Your marital status can be single, married, separated, divorced, or widowed.
4. Write your address. You will have to fit the house number and street and the city and state on this one line, so write small and abbreviate if you can. For example, write "St." for street, "Ave." for avenue, and "E." for east.
5. Include your area code when you write your home phone number.
6. Write the kind of work that you do, such as plumber or secretary.
7. Write the name of the company you work for.
8. When you write your business address, write small and abbreviate, the way you did for item 4.
9. Include your area code when you write your work phone number.
10. Write the name of your husband or wife.
11. Write the name of the insurance company that provides you with health insurance. If you have Medicaid or Medicare, write that.
12. Write your medical insurance policy number.
13. Usually, people find out about doctors from friends, relatives, coworkers, or other doctors. Write the name of the person who told you about this doctor.
14. Write the name of the doctor you used to go to before you found this doctor.
15. Write the name of the person you would want to be contacted in an emergency.
16. Write this person's telephone number, including the area code.
17. Answer each question in this section of the form by checking the Yes or No box. Also, write in answers when they are asked for. If you are not sure about an answer, ask the doctor's assistant to help you.
18. Sign your name and write today's date all in numbers.
19. Do not write in this section of the form.

Fill Out the Medical History

Using your own personal information, fill out the medical history. You can leave the Referred By area blank. If you do not have health insurance, you can leave the Medical Insurance Company part of the form blank also.

① Date _____

Full name _____ ② Birth date _____ Marital status _____ ③

④ Home address _____ Zip _____ Home phone _____ ⑤

⑥ Occupation _____ ⑦ Employer _____ Social security no. _____

⑧ Business address _____ Zip _____ Work phone _____ ⑨

⑩ Name of spouse _____ Occupation _____ Employer _____

⑪ Medical insurance company _____ Policy no. _____ ⑫

⑬ Referred by _____ Previous doctor _____ ⑭

⑮ In case of emergency, contact _____ Phone no. _____ ⑯

⑰

                                                                                                           YES NO

1. Have you ever been hospitalized, had major operations, or had serious illnesses? .... ☐ ☐

    If so, explain _____

2. Are you under any medical treatment now? .... ☐ ☐
3. Have you had any allergic reactions to any drugs, including penicillin, codeine, novocaine, aspirin? .... ☐ ☐
4. Has there been a change in your health in the past year? .... ☐ ☐
5. Have you ever had a blood transfusion? .... ☐ ☐
6. Have you ever had kidney dialysis treatment? .... ☐ ☐
7. Have you ever had abnormal bleeding problems after a cut or tooth extraction? .... ☐ ☐
8. Are you now taking drugs or medications? .... ☐ ☐

    If so, what? _____

9. Has a physician ever informed you that you had:

	YES	NO		YES	NO
Heart ailment	☐	☐	Liver disease	☐	☐
High blood pressure	☐	☐	Venereal disease	☐	☐
Rheumatic fever	☐	☐	AIDS or HIV	☐	☐
Heart murmur	☐	☐	Stomach or intestinal disease	☐	☐
Angina	☐	☐	Kidney disease	☐	☐
Stroke	☐	☐	Tumors or growths	☐	☐
Blood disease	☐	☐	Diabetes	☐	☐
Hemophilia	☐	☐	Tuberculosis	☐	☐
Asthma	☐	☐	Respiratory disease	☐	☐
Hepatitis or yellow jaundice	☐	☐	Epilepsy	☐	☐

10. Women: A. Are you pregnant? .... ☐ ☐

    B. Estimated date of delivery _____

⑲ Medical history summary

⑱ Signature _____

Date _____

Blood pressure:

60 CHAPTER 3 MEDICAL FORMS

LESSON 15

Application for Medicaid

Medicaid is a kind of government assistance that pays for medical and health services, such as doctor visits, medical tests, prescription drugs, and hospital expenses. Only people who earn below a certain income and who have no other resources can receive medicaid. The medicaid application asks for a lot of information. In addition to filling out the application, people who apply for medicaid must be interviewed by someone from their local medicaid office.

The application for medicaid is also used by people applying for food stamps, public assistance (welfare), and other services provided by the government. In this lesson, you will not fill out the parts of the form that relate to these services.

▶ Be Prepared

The application for medicaid is long and asks for a lot of information. You will be able to fill it out at home, so you will not have to bring all the information with you when you go to the medicaid office.

Here is a list of some of the information you will have to provide on the form:

- Personal information about you and all the people who live with you, including maiden names and social security numbers.
- Sources and amount of income for you and everyone who lives with you.
- Financial information about you and everyone who lives with you.

Many of the questions on the application are about the people who live with you. You will have to ask them for the information you need to fill out the form. You and everyone who lives with you and is over 18 years of age must sign the form and provide information about citizenship.

Application for Medicaid Vocabulary

boarder (lodger)   A person who pays another for food and shelter.

certification   A statement saying that something is true and accurate.

deceased   Dead.

eligible   Meeting the requirements for approval.

maiden name   A woman's name before she was married.

minor children   Children under 18 years of age.

pending eviction   Awaiting the completion of the legal process that forces a tenant to leave the place where he or she lives.

perjury   Swearing to something that is not true.

verification   Proof of truth or accuracy.

It is not possible to list here all the difficult or unfamiliar words that appear on the application. If you are not sure of what a word means, you can look in a dictionary or ask someone at the medicaid office to help you.

How to Fill Out the Application for Medicaid

The following hints will help you fill out the application. The numbers and letters in the following list match the circled numbers and letters on the application. Some parts of the application do not have circled numbers or letters. You should be able to fill in these parts of the application without any special hints or explanation.

Do not write in any of the shaded sections or areas of the form.

PAGE 1

1. The medicaid office will send you notices or letters. If you want to receive them in both Spanish and English, check the first box. If you want to receive them in English only, check the second box.

2. *M.I.* stands for "middle initial."

3. Your marital status can be single, married, divorced, separated, or widowed. Write the one that applies to you.

4. If your mail is sent to someone who receives it for you, write the name the mail is addressed to.

5. Your phone bill is different from month to month. Write the amount that it usually is.

6. If your mail is sent to an address that is different from the address you wrote on the form, such as a post office box, write the mailing address here.

7. You must apply for medicaid through a government agency. Write the name of the agency that is helping you.

8. Write the name of the person at the government agency who is helping you.

9. Write the person's phone number.

10. Write the address of the place you lived before you moved to where you live now.

PAGE ONE

CENTER/OFFICE	APPLICATION DATE	UNIT	(UNIT) WORKER	DIST	CASE TYPE	SERV IND	CASE NUMBER	REGISTRY NUMBER	VERS

CASE NAME	DISTRICT	NO. REUSE INDICATOR	SUFFIX	FS SUFFIX	CATEGORY	LANG.	ETHNIC

EFFECTIVE DATE	DISPOSITION (DENIAL, REASON CODE, WITHDRAWAL)	EXTRA PAGES SFED/T	SERVICES TRANSACTION TYPE (NEW OPENING 02, REOPEN 10, RECERTIFICATON 06)	SEPARATE DET CODE	REASON CODE	FORM ___ OF ___

I CONSENT TO WITHDRAW MY APPLICATION
SIGNATURE _____ DATE _____

ELIGIBILITY DETERMINED BY (WORKER):	DATE	ELIGIBILITY APPROVED BY (SUPERVISOR):	DATE

SIGNATURE OF PERSON WHO OBTAINED ELIGIBILITY INFORMATION X _____	DATE	EMPLOYED BY: ☐ PROVIDER AGENCY SPECIFY: _____ ☐ SOCIAL SERVICES DISTRICT

DSS-2921 (NYC) (Rev. 7/91)

NEW YORK STATE DEPARTMENT OF SOCIAL SERVICES

APPLICATION FOR: PUBLIC ASSISTANCE - MEDICAL ASSISTANCE - FOOD STAMPS - SERVICES

PLEASE PRINT CLEARLY - DO NOT WRITE IN SHADED AREAS

(1) DO YOU WANT TO RECEIVE NOTICES IN: ☐ SPANISH AND ENGLISH ☐ ENGLISH ONLY

FIRST NAME | **(2)** M.I. | LAST NAME | **(3)** MARITAL STATUS

HOUSE NO. | ST. ADDRESS | APT. NO. | CITY | COUNTY | STATE | ZIP CODE

(4) CARE OF NAME (Complete if you receive your mail in care of another person) | AREA CODE PHONE NO. | **(5)** PHONE BILL AMT.

(6) MAILING ADDRESS (If different from above) | APT. NO. | CITY | COUNTY | STATE | ZIP CODE

(7) AGENCY HELPING APPLICANT APPLY | **(8)** CONTACT PERSON | AREA CODE PHONE NO. **(9)**

(10) FORMER ADDRESS | APT. NO. | CITY | COUNTY | STATE | ZIP CODE

HOW LONG HAVE YOU LIVED AT YOUR PRESENT ADDRESS? | YEARS | MONTHS | **(11)** ANOTHER PHONE WHERE YOU CAN BE REACHED | NAME | AREA CODE PHONE NO.

IF YOU ARE APPLYING FOR FOOD STAMPS
- You can file this application the same day you receive it; if eligible, benefits are provided back to the filing date of application.
- We must accept your application if, at a minimum, it contains your Name, Address (if you have one), and Signature in this box.
- You do not have to be interviewed before you file an application.
- If you are applying for both Cash Assistance and Food Stamps, usually you will only be required to have a single interview for both programs.

(12) APPLICANT/REPRESENTATIVE SIGNATURE X | DATE SIGNED

(13) CHECK WHICH PROGRAMS YOU ARE APPLYING FOR: ☐ CASH ASSISTANCE ☐ MEDICAL ASSISTANCE 20 ☐ MEDICARE BUY-IN ☐ FOOD STAMPS ☐ SERVICES 40

NEED FOOD STAMPS RIGHT AWAY...You may be eligible for EXPEDITED FOOD STAMP SERVICE.
If your household has little or no income or liquid resources, **or** if your rent and utility expenses are more than your income and liquid resources, **or** if you do not have any place of your own in which to live, you may be eligible to receive Food Stamps within a few days. Your worker will review your circumstances to see if you are eligible for these benefits.

(14) DO YOU HAVE ANY OF THESE PROBLEMS?
☐ FUEL OR UTILITY SHUTOFF ☐ URGENT PERSONAL OR FAMILY PROBLEM ☐ SERIOUS MEDICAL PROBLEM ☐ NO PLACE TO STAY/HOMELESS
☐ PENDING EVICTION ☐ RECENTLY LOST INCOME ☐ NO FOOD ☐ OTHER

(15) IF THE HUSBAND OR WIFE OF ANYONE APPLYING LIVES SOMEPLACE ELSE. PLEASE INDICATE BELOW. (Include name and date of birth even if deceased)

FIRST NAME	M.I.	LAST NAME	**(16)** DATE OF BIRTH	SOCIAL SECURITY NO.

ADDRESS	CITY	COUNTY	STATE	ZIP CODE

IF ANYONE WHO IS UNDER 21 AND APPLYING HAS A PARENT WHO LIVES SOMEPLACE ELSE. PLEASE LIST BELOW. (Include name and date of birth even if deceased)

(17)

PARENT'S NAME	ADDRESS	DATE OF BIRTH	SOCIAL SECURITY NO.	NAME OF PERSON UNDER 21

11. If you can be called at a phone number other than the one you wrote on the third line of the application, write the name of the person to ask for at that number and then that person's phone number.

12. This section relates to food stamps only. You can skip this section.

13. Check the box for Medical Assistance, which means that you are applying for medicaid.

14. Check the box or boxes relating to problems you might have.

15. If your husband or wife does not live with you, fill out the information requested about that person.

16. Write your husband's or wife's date of birth all in numbers. For example, if his or her birth date is November 23, 1959, write "11/23/59."

17. If you or anyone in your household applying for medicaid is under 21 years of age and has a parent or parents who live somewhere else, fill in the information about the parent or parents.

PAGE 2

18. All the information you will write on this line of the form is about you.

    a. The question here is "Is this person applying?" Since you are applying for medicaid, put a check mark in the Yes column.

    b. Write your date of birth all in numbers. If your birth date is July 9, 1965, write 7 in the Month box, "9" in the Day box, and "65" in the Year box.

    c. Write "M" for *male* or "F" for *female*.

    d. This box is already filled out for you. Do not write anything else.

    e. This questions asks whether the person referred to on this line of the form buys food or prepares meals with you. This line of the form refers to you, so put a check mark in the Yes box.

19. All the other lines on this section of the form relate to people who live with you. You must provide all the information requested about these people, even if they are not applying for medicaid.

    f. If the person named is applying for medicaid, put a check mark in the Yes box. If this person is not applying for medicaid, check No.

    g. Write this person's date of birth all in numbers.

    h. Write this person's relationship to you, for example, wife, husband, son, daughter, nephew, cousin, friend, or boarder.

PAGE TWO

LIST EVERYBODY WHO LIVES WITH YOU, EVEN IF THEY ARE NOT APPLYING WITH YOU. PLEASE PRINT.

DOES THIS PERSON (INCLUDING YOUR MINOR CHILDREN) BUY FOOD AND/OR PREPARE MEALS WITH YOU?

LIST **YOUR** NAME FIRST   (Middle Initial)   IS THIS PERSON APPLYING?

LN	RI or Suffix	FIRST NAME	M.I.	LAST NAME	YES	NO	MONTH	DAY	YEAR	SEX M or F	RELATIONSHIP TO YOU	SOCIAL SECURITY NUMBERS OF APPLYING MEMBERS	YES	NO
01					*a*		*b*			*c*	*d* SELF		*e*	
02					*f*		*g*				*h*	*i*	*j*	
03														
04														
05														
06														
07														
08														
09														
10														

PLEASE LIST MAIDEN OR OTHER NAMES OF PEOPLE LISTED ABOVE

LnNo	ONC	FIRST NAME	M.I.	LAST NAME

INCOME — ANSWERS ALL QUESTIONS LISTED BELOW.

INDICATE IF **YOU OR ANYONE WHO LIVES WITH YOU** RECEIVES MONEY FROM:	YES	NO	*b* IF YES, GIVE AMOUNT/VALUE	*c* WHO	*d* IF YES, GIVE AMOUNT/VALUE	*e* WHO	CD
WAGES, SALARY, INCLUDING OVERTIME, COMMISSIONS, TRAINING PROGRAMS, TIPS	*a*		$		$		01
SELF-EMPLOYMENT							20
PUBLIC ASSISTANCE GRANT							37
CHILD SUPPORT PAYMENTS (RECEIVED)							06
UNEMPLOYMENT INSURANCE BENEFITS							49
SUPPLEMENTAL SECURITY INCOME (SS) BENEFITS							45
SOCIAL SECURITY DISABILITY BENEFITS							42
SOCIAL SECURITY DEPENDENT BENEFITS							
SOCIAL SECURITY SURVIVOR'S BENEFITS							43
SOCIAL SECURITY RETIREMENT BENEFITS							44
RAILROAD RETIREMENT BENEFITS							38
RETIREMENT BENEFITS (PENSIONS)							39
VETERAN'S PENSIONS/BENEFITS/AID AND ATTENDANCE							55
GI DEPENDENCY ALLOTMENTS							10
NYS DISABILITY BENEFITS							33
PRIVATE DISABILITY INSURANCE-HEALTH/ACCIDENT INSURANCE POLICY INCOME							
WORKER'S COMPENSATION							59
EDUCATION GRANTS OR LOANS							
UNION BENEFITS (INCLUDING STRIKE BENEFITS)							50
RENTAL INCOME (RECEIVED)							31
BOARDERS/LODGERS INCOME (RECEIVED)							14
CONTRIBUTIONS/GIFTS (RECEIVED)							
LOANS (RECEIVED)							
ALIMONY/SUPPORT (RECEIVED)							02
NO FAULT INSURANCE BENEFITS							
DIVIDENDS/INTEREST FROM STOCKS, BONDS, SAVINGS, ETC.							03
OTHER INCOME (Please Specify)							

LESSON 15   APPLICATION FOR MEDICAID

i. If this person is applying for medicaid, write his or her social security number. If this person is not applying for medicaid, it is not necessary to provide the social security number.

j. If this person buys foods or prepares meals with you, check the Yes box. If this person does neither of these things, check No.

20. If any of the people listed in items 18 and 19 are women with married names, give their full maiden names here. If any of the people in items 18 or 19 use names other than their legal names written above, write those other names here.

21. This part of the form concerns your income and the income of the people who live with you.

a. Read the items in the left column. If you or anyone who lives with you receives money from one or more of the items listed, check Yes on the appropriate line. If the answer is no, check No and go on to the next line.

b. If you answered yes to any of the items in 21a, write the amount of money received. This amount should be the total for a whole year.

c. If you are the person who receives the money, write "Self." If someone who lives with you receives the money, write who that person is.

d. If more than one person receives money, write the amount the second person receives.

e. If more than one person receives money, write who the second person is.

PAGE 3

22. Before you can fill out the information in the top section of this form, you must read and be sure that you understand the certification, which is in the middle of the page. The certification says that if you sign this section of the form, you are swearing that you are a citizen or national of the United States or an alien with legal immigration status. The information you provide on the form will be sent to the Immigration and Naturalization Service.

You do not have to write anything in this section.

23. You and all the people who live with you must sign this section of the form. However, if you live with someone who does not have legal immigration status, that person should not sign this section of the form, because the certification states that people signing are citizens or legal aliens.

Each person must sign the form and then fill out the rest of the line:

a. Write the date all in numbers.

PAGE THREE

DO NOT SIGN UNTIL YOU READ AND UNDERSTAND THE CERTIFICATION BELOW.

- IF YOU ARE APPLYING **ONLY** FOR FOOD STAMPS OR **ONLY** FOR SERVICES, YOU DO NOT NEED TO COMPLETE THIS SECTION.
- IF YOU ARE AN UNDOCUMENTED ALIEN APPLYING **ONLY** FOR MEDICAL ASSISTANCE BENEFITS AS A RESULT OF AN EMERGENCY MEDICAL CONDITION, YOU DO NOT NEED TO COMPLETE THIS SECTION.
- IF YOU ARE APPLYING **ONLY** FOR MEDICAL ASSISTANCE AND YOU ARE PREGNANT, YOU DO NOT NEED TO COMPLETE THIS SECTION
- IF YOU HAVE QUESTIONS, SEE THE "HOW TO COMPLETE" INSTRUCTIONS.

LN	SIGNATURES	a. DATE SIGNED MO. / DAY / YEAR	b. CHECK ONE FOR EACH PERSON	c. ALIEN NUMBER (If Known)
01	SIGN NAME X		☐ CITIZEN/NATIONAL ☐ ALIEN	
02	SIGN NAME X		☐ CITIZEN/NATIONAL ☐ ALIEN	
03	SIGN NAME X		☐ CITIZEN/NATIONAL ☐ ALIEN	
04	SIGN NAME X		☐ CITIZEN/NATIONAL ☐ ALIEN	
05	SIGN NAME X		☐ CITIZEN/NATIONAL ☐ ALIEN	
06	SIGN NAME X		☐ CITIZEN/NATIONAL ☐ ALIEN	
07	SIGN NAME X		☐ CITIZEN/NATIONAL ☐ ALIEN	
08	SIGN NAME X		☐ CITIZEN/NATIONAL ☐ ALIEN	
09	SIGN NAME X		☐ CITIZEN/NATIONAL ☐ ALIEN	
10	SIGN NAME X		☐ CITIZEN/NATIONAL ☐ ALIEN	

SIGNATURE OF WITNESS	DATE SIGNED

I WITNESSED THE MARKS MADE IN LINES ___ , ___ , ___ , ___ , ___ .

CERTIFICATON OF CITIZENSHIP / ALIEN STATUS
I CERTIFY, UNDER THE PENALTY OF PERJURY, BY SIGNING MY NAME ABOVE, THAT I, AND/OR THE PERSONS FOR WHOM I AM SIGNING, AM A UNITED STATES CITIZEN OR NATIONAL OF THE UNITED STATES OR AN ALIEN WITH SATISFACTORY IMMIGRATION STATUS. I UNDERSTAND THAT INFORMATION ABOUT ME WILL BE SUBMITTED TO THE IMMIGRATION AND NATURALIZATION SERVICE FOR VERIFICATION OF MY IMMIGRATION STATUS, IF APPLICABLE. I FURTHER UNDERSTAND THAT THE USE OR DISCLOSURE OF INFORMATION ABOUT ME IS RESTRICTED TO PERSONS AND ORGANIZATIONS DIRECTLY CONNECTED WITH THE VERIFICATION OF IMMIGRATION STATUS AND THE ADMINISTRATION OR ENFORCEMENT OF THE PROVISIONS OF THE PUBLIC ASSISTANCE AND MEDICAL ASSISTANCE PROGRAMS.

After you read this certification, sign above in the space(s) provided. If an applicant cannot sign his or her name, the applicant must make his or her mark ("X") in the space provided. The mark must be made in front of a witness. The witness should sign in the witness space provided above.

IS ANYONE IN YOUR HOUSEHOLD AN ALIEN WHO WAS SPONSORED FOR ADMISSION INTO THE U.S. WITHIN THE PAST THREE YEARS?	YES ☐	NO ☐	WHAT IS THE NAME OF THE SPONSOR OR SPONSORING ORGANIZATION?

RESOURCES — ANSWERS ALL QUESTIONS LISTED BELOW.

INDICATE IF **YOU OR ANYONE WHO LIVES WITH YOU** WHO IS APPLYING:	YES	NO	IF YES, GIVE AMOUNT/VALUE	WHO	IF YES, GIVE AMOUNT/VALUE	WHO
HAS CASH ON HAND			$		$	
HAS A CHECKING ACCOUNT(S)						
HAS A SAVINGS ACCOUNT(S) OR C.D. (CERT. OF DEPOSIT)						
HAS A CREDIT UNION ACCOUNT(S)						
HAS AN "IN-TRUST" OR P.A.S.S. ACCOUNT(S)						
HAS SAVINGS BONDS						
HAS STOCKS, BONDS, CERTIFICATES OR MUTUAL FUNDS						
HAS LIFE INSURANCE						
HAS A BURIAL TRUST/BURIAL FUND						
HAS A BURIAL SPACE						
HAS AN IRA, KEOGH, 401-K OR DEFERRED COMPENSATION ACCOUNT(S)						
HAS AN ANNUITY						
IS NAMED THE BENEFICIARY OF A TRUST						
EXPECTS TO RECEIVE A TRUST FUND, LAWSUIT SETTLEMENT, INHERITANCE OR INCOME FROM ANY OTHER SOURCES						
IS ELIGIBLE FOR AN INCOME TAX REFUND						
HAS A SAFE DEPOSIT BOX						
HAS OWN HOME						
HAS REAL ESTATE INCLUDING INCOME-PRODUCING AND NON-INCOME-PRODUCING PROPERTY						
HAS A MOTOR VEHICLE(S) OR OTHER VEHICLE(S) (Specify) YEAR ____ MAKE/MODEL _____ YEAR ____ MAKE/MODEL _____						
HAS RESOURCES OTHER THAN THOSE LISTED ABOVE						
HAS ANYONE (INCLUDING YOUR SPOUSE EVEN IF NOT APPLYING OR LIVING WITH YOU) SOLD/TRANSFERRED/GIVEN AWAY ANY CASH, REAL ESTATE OR PERSONAL PROPERTY IN THE PAST 30 MONTHS? IF YES, WHEN? _____						

LESSON 15   APPLICATION FOR MEDICAID

b. Check whether you (and each of them) are a citizen/national or a legal alien.

c. The legal aliens must write their alien numbers, with each number between the tick marks.

24. If someone lives with you and is a citizen or a legal alien but cannot write his or her name, that person should put a mark on this line. Someone else must be present when the person writes the mark and must sign the form as a witness that the mark was made. This person should also write the date the mark was made all in numbers.

25. This question is very similar to item 21 on page 2 of the form. Follow the instructions for item 21 in filling out this section.

PAGE 4

26. There are two sections on this part of the form, one on the right side of the page and one on the left. In each section, there are questions in the left column. Read the questions in each of the left columns carefully. If your answer is yes to the question, check the Yes box (a) and then answer the question in the right column (c). If your answer to the question in the left column is no, check the No box (b) and go on to the next question. You do not have to write anything in the right column (c) if you answered no.

27. If you are now receiving any form of public assistance or if you have ever received any in the past, fill in this part. Write the kind of assistance you received in the left column, the place (city and state) where you received it, and the date (all in numbers) when you last received it.

28. The form says that you do not have to answer this question—it is optional. However, it also says that if you do not answer, the person who interviews you will fill out the answer. If you want to answer this question, check the box that applies to you.

PAGE 5

All of page 5 is filled out by the medicaid worker. You do not have to write anything. Therefore, this page is not shown.

PAGE 6

The only thing you have to do on this page is sign your name and write the date at the bottom. You should, however, read everything on the page. If you do not understand something, you can ask someone at the medicaid office to explain things to you.

Most of what this page says is that the information you provided on the form is the truth.

ANSWERS ALL QUESTIONS LISTED BELOW.

SHELTER (HOUSING) EXPENSES

	YES (a)	NO (b)	IF YES, GIVE AMOUNT (c)
DO YOU (OR ANYONE WHO LIVES WITH YOU) HAVE A RENT, MORTGAGE OR OTHER SHELTER EXPENSE?			$
DO YOU (OR ANYONE WHO LIVES WITH YOU) HAVE A HEAT BILL SEPARATE FROM YOUR RENT OR MORTGAGE?			
DO YOU (OR ANYONE WHO LIVES WITH YOU) HAVE THE FOLLOWING EXPENSES SEPARATE FROM YOUR RENT OR MORTGAGE?			
• ELECTRICITY			
• GAS			
• OTHER UTILITIES (WATER, ETC.)			
• TELEPHONE			
• AIR CONDITIONING			
• UTILITY/TELEPHONE INSTALLATION FEES			
DOES ANY PERSON, GROUP OR ORGANIZATION OUTSIDE THE HOUSEHOLD PAY ANY OF THE HOUSEHOLD EXPENSES?			
DO YOU LIVE IN SECTION 8 OR OTHER SUBSIDIZED HOUSING? IF YES, ARE YOU IN THE CERTIFICATE PROGRAM?			
DO YOU LIVE IN PUBLIC HOUSING?			

HEALTH / MEDICAL

INDICATE IF YOU OR ANYONE WHO LIVES WITH YOU WHO IS APPLYING:	YES	NO	IF YES, WHO
HAS ANY MEDICAL BILLS OR MEDICALLY-RELATED EXPENSES			
HAS PAID OR UNPAID MEDICAL BILLS FOR THE THREE MONTHS PRECEDING THE MONTH OF THIS APPLICATION			
HAS HEALTH OR HOSPITAL/ACCIDENT INSURANCE			
HAS MEDICARE (RED, WHITE, AND BLUE CARD)			
HAS A HEALTH ATTENDANT			
IS BLIND, SICK OR DISABLED			
IS A HANDICAPPED CHILD			
IS IN A HOSPITAL, NURSING HOME OR OTHER MEDICAL INSTITUTION			
IS PREGNANT			
IS DRUG OR ALCOHOL DEPENDENT			
RECEIVES TREATMENT FROM DRUG ABUSE OR ALCOHOL TREATMENT PROGRAM			

OTHER EXPENSES

INDICATE IF YOU OR ANYONE WHO LIVES WITH YOU WHO IS APPLYING:	YES	NO	IF YES, GIVE AMOUNT
PAYS TUITION AND FEES			$
HAS CHILD OR DEPENDENT CARE EXPENSES			
PAYS CHILD SUPPORT OR ALIMONY			
HAS ADDITIONAL EXPENSES SPECIFY _____			
BUYS OR PLANS TO BUY MEALS FROM A HOME DELIVERY OR COMMUNAL DINING SERVICE			
ARE YOU ABLE TO PREPARE MEALS AT HOME?			

I HAVE ☐   HAVE NOT ☐   SOLD, TRANSFERRED OR GIVEN AWAY ANY OF MY PROPERTY TO ANYONE TO GET PUBLIC ASSISTANCE, MEDICAL ASSISTANCE OR FOOD STAMPS.

BE SURE TO READ AND SIGN THIS APPLICATION ON PAGE SIX.

EMPLOYMENT / TRAINING

INDICATE IF YOU OR ANYONE WHO LIVES WITH YOU WHO IS APPLYING:	YES (a)	NO (b)	IF YES, WHO (c)
IS PARTICIPATING IN A STRIKE			
IS 16 YEARS OF AGE OR OLDER AND IS ATTENDING SCHOOL, COLLEGE OR AN APPROVED TRAINING PROGRAM			
IS A MIGRANT OR SEASONAL FARM WORKER			

ADDITIONAL INFORMATION REQUIRED

	YES	NO	IF YES, WHO
HAVE YOUR OR ANYONE WHO LIVES WITH YOU WHO IS APPLYING MOVED INTO NEW YORK STATE WITHIN THE PAST TWELVE MONTHS?			
HAVE YOU OR ANYONE WHO LIVES WITH YOU WHO IS APPLYING MOVED INTO THIS COUNTY FROM ANOTHER NEW YORK STATE COUNTY WITHIN THE PAST TWO MONTHS?			
DOES THE STEP-PARENT OF ANY CHILDREN WHO LIVE WITH YOU HAVE ANY RESOURCES OR RECEIVE INCOME OF ANY KIND?			
ARE YOU OR ANYONE WHO LIVES WITH YOU A U.S. ARMED FORCES VETERAN OR WIDOW, SPOUSE, CHILD OR MOTHER OF A U.S. VETERAN?			
HAVE YOU OR ANYONE WHO LIVES WITH YOU RECEIVED BENEFITS FOR WHICH THEY WERE NOT ENTITLED, WHICH HAVE NOT BEEN FULLY REPAID TO THIS OR ANOTHER AGENCY?			
HAVE YOU OR ANYONE WHO LIVES WITH YOU EVER BEEN FOUND GUILTY OF AND/OR BEEN DISQUALIFIED FOR FOOD STAMP FRAUD/ INTENTIONAL PROGRAM VIOLATION?			
DO YOU OR DOES ANYONE WHO LIVES WITH YOU NOW RECEIVE ANY TYPE OF ASSISTANCE OR SERVICES OUTSIDE OF NEW YORK CITY?			
DO YOU OR DOES ANYONE WHO LIVES WITH YOU NOW RECEIVE ANY TYPE OF ASSISTANCE OR SERVICES OUTSIDE OF NEW YORK STATE?			
HAVE YOU OR ANYONE WHO LIVES WITH YOU APPLIED FOR OR RECEIVED ANY TYPE OF ASSISTANCE OR SERVICES OUTSIDE OF NEW YORK CITY IN THE PAST SIX MONTHS?			
HAVE YOU OR ANYONE WHO LIVES WITH YOU APPLIED FOR OR RECEIVED ANY TYPE OF ASSISTANCE OR SERVICES OUTSIDE OF NEW YORK STATE IN THE PAST SIX MONTHS?			

LN	TYPE OF ASSISTANCE	WHERE	DATE OF LAST ASSISTANCE

NON-DISCRIMINATION NOTICE

This application will be considered without regard to race, color, sex, handicaps, religious creed, national origin or political beliefs.

RACE / ETHNIC AFFILIATION FOR APPLICANT ONLY

(Completion is optional. However, if not completed, the interviewer may have to record it by observation. This information is being collected only to be sure that everyone receives food stamps and/or assistance/care on a fair basis. This information will not affect your eligibility.)

I AM
(CHECK ONLY ONE)

B ☐ Black not of Hispanic origin
H ☐ Hispanic
A ☐ Asian or Pacific Islander
I ☐ American Indian or Alaskan Native
W ☐ White not of Hispanic origin

SUPPORT - Any person making application for or those in receipt of Aid to Dependent Children (ADC) or foster care services shall know that such application for or receipt of ADC or foster care services shall operate as an assignment to the State and the Social Services district concerned, of any rights to support from any other person, as such applicant or recipient may have in his own behalf or any other family member for whom the applicant or recipient is applying for or receiving assistance. (Social Services Law 348)

SOCIAL SERRCURITY NUMBER (SSN) - A person making application for Public Assistance (PA), for Medical Assistance (MA) or for Food Stamps (FS) shall disclose the SSN of any person for whom PA or MA or FS is requested, except when the individual is an alien seeking MA-only for the treatment of an emergency medical condition. Such disclosure is mandatory for PA under the authority of Section 351.2 of Title 18 of the Official Compilation of Codes, Rules and Regulations of the State of New York (18NYCRR) and 42 USC 602(a) (25), for MA under the authority of 18NYCRR Sections 351.2 and 360-1.2 of Title 18 of the Offical Compilation of Codes, Rules and Regulations of the State of New York and 42 USC 1320b-7 and for FS under the authority of Section 1327 of the Public Law 97-98 and 7 CFR 273.2 SSNs are used to provide proper identification of applicants for and recipients of PA, MA and FS and to verify income, eligibility and benefit amounts. We will also be using your SSN to match with IRS unearned income data and with the New York State Department of Labor for unemployment insurance information and with the New York State Department of Taxation and Finance for earned income data.

CONSENT - I understand that by signing this application/certification form I agree to any investigation made by the Department of Social Services to verify or confirm the information I have given or any other investigation made by them in connection with my request for PA, MA, FS or Services. If additional information is requested, I will provide it. I will also cooperate fully with State and Federal personnel in a Food Stamp Quality Control Review.

CHANGES - I agree to inform the agency **promptly** of any change in my needs, income, property, living arrangements or address to the best of my knowledge or belief.

ASSIGNMENT OF INSURANCE AND OTHER BENEFITS - For PA and MA, I will file any claims for health or accident insurance benefits or any other resources to which I am entitled, and do hereby assign by such resources to the Social Services official to whom this application is made. In addition, I will assist in making any required assignment of benefits or resources to the Social Services official to whom this application is made.

DIRECT PAYMENT - I authorize that payment to me or members of my household for health or accident insurance benefits be made directly to the appropriate Social Services official for medical and other health services furnished while we are eligible for MA.

MEDICARE - I authorize payments under "Medicare" (Part B of Title XVIII, Supplementary Medical Insurance Program) to be made directly to physicians and medical suppliers on any future unpaid bills for medical and other health services furnished to me while I am eligible for MA.

PENALTIES - I understand that my application may be investigated, and I agree to cooperate in such an investigation. Federal and State law provide for penalties of fine, imprisonment or both if you do not tell the truth when you apply for PA and/or MA benefits or at any time when you are questioned about eligibility, or cause someone else not to tell the truth regarding your application or your continuing eligibility. Penalties also apply if you conceal or fail to disclose facts regarding your initial and continuing eligibility for PA and/or MA or if you conceal or fail to disclose facts that would affect the right of someone for whom you have applied to obtain or continue to receive PA and/or MA benefits; and such benefits must be used for that other person and not for yourself.

Federal and State law provide that any transfer of resource for less than fair market value made by an individual or his/her spouse within or after the thirty months immediately preceding the date the individual becomes institutionalized, or the date of application for MA as an institutionalized person, if later, **may** render the individual ineligible for nursing facility services for up to thirty months. This provision applies only to transfers made on or after October 1, 1989.

FOOD STAMP PENALTY WARNING - THE INFORMATION PROVIDED ON THIS FORM WILL BE SUBJECT TO VERIFICATION BY FEDERAL, STATE AND LOCAL OFFICIALS. IF ANY IS FOUND INACCURATE, YOU MAY BE DENIED FS AND/OR BE SUBJECT TO CRIMINAL PROSECUTION FOR KNOWINGLY PROVIDING FALSE INFORMATION. ANY MEMBER OF YOUR HOUSEHOLD WHO INTENTIONALLY BREAKS ANY OF THE FOLLOWING RULES CAN BE BARRED FROM THE FS PROGRAM FOR 6 MONTHS AFTER THE FIRST VIOLATION, 12 MONTHS AFTER THE SECOND VIOLATION, AND PERMANENTLY AFTER THE THIRD VIOLATION. THE INDIVIDUAL CAN BE FINED UP TO $10,000, IMPRISONED UP TO 5 YEARS, OR BOTH. A COURT CAN ALSO BAR AN INDIVIDUAL FOR AN ADDITIONAL 18 MONTHS FROM THE FS PROGRAM. THE INDIVIDUAL MAY ALSO BE SUBJECT TO FURTHER PROSECUTION UNDER OTHER APPLICABLE FEDERAL LAWS.

DO NOT give false information, or hide information to get or continue to get FS. **DO NOT** trade or sell FS or food stamp indentification/benefit cards for your household.
DO NOT alter food stamp indentification/benefit cards to get FS you're not entitled to receive. **DO NOT** use FS to buy ineligible items such as alcohol drinks and tobacco.
DO NOT use someone else's FS or food stamp indentification/benefit cards for your household.

In signing this application, I certify, under penalty of perjury, that the information contained in this application is correct and complete to the best of my knowledge.

PICK UP YOUR FOOD STAMPS DURING THE PERIOD OF INTENDED USE - You or your authorized representative must pick up your household's food stamp coupons at an authorized issuance site within the time period the benefits are authorized to cover. Benefits issued between the 1st and 20th day of a month will be available for pick-up until the last day of that month. Benefits issued after the 20th day will be available until the last day of the next month. Benefits not picked up cannot be replaced.

FOOD STAMP AUTHORIZED REPRESENTATIVE - You can authorize someone who knows your household circumstances to **apply** for FS for you. If you do, have them **sign** in the Signature section at the bottom. You can also authorize someone outside your household to get FS for you or to use them to buy food for you. If you would like to authorize someone, print the person's name directly below.

NAME AND ADDRESS OF AUTHORIZED REPRESENTATIVE (PLEASE PRINT)		PHONE NUMBER

CERTIFICATION OF CITIZENSHIP/ALIEN STATUS FOR FOOD STAMPS - I SWEAR AND AFFIRM, UNDER PENALTIES OF PERJURY, THAT ALL HOUSEHOLD MEMBERS INCLUDING MYSELF WHO ARE APPLYING FOR OR RECEIVING FS ARE UNITED STATES (U.S) CITIZENS OR U.S. NATIONALS OR PERSONS WITH SATISFACTORY IMMIGRATION STATUS. I UNDERSTAND THAT INFORMATION ABOUT MY FOOD STAMP HOUSEHOLD WILL BE SUBMITTED TO THE IMMIGRATION AND NATURALIZATION SERVICE (INS) FOR VERIFICATION OF IMMIGRATION STATUS, IF APPLICABLE. I FURTHER UNDERSTAND THAT THE USE OR DISCLOSURE OF INFORMATION ABOUT ALL HOUSEHOLD MEMBERS INCLUDING MYSELF WHO ARE APPLYING FOR OR RECEIVING FS IS RESTRICTED TO PERSONS AND ORGANIZATIONS DIRECTLY CONNECTED WITH THE VERIFICATION OF IMMIGRATION STATUS AND THE ADMINISTRATION OR ENFORCEMENT OF PROVISIONS OF THE FOOD STAMP PROGRAM. I ALSO UNDERSTAND THAT INFORMATION RECEIVED FROM THE INS MAY AFFECT MY HOUSEHOLD'S ELIGIBILITY AND LEVEL OF BENEFITS.

Authorization for Reimbursement of Public Assistance Benefits from SSI Retroactive Payment - I authorize the Secretary of the United States Department of Health and Human Services, through the Social Security Administration (SSA), to send to the local social services district the amount due to me at the time of my first payment of (1) retroactive Supplemental Security Income (SSI) benefits that I may receive upon an application for SSI or (2) retroactive SSI benefits I may receive if I am terminated or suspended from receiving SSI benefits and am later reinstated.

I understand that the local social services district may take from my SSI payment the amount of Public Assistance (except assistance paid wholly or partly with federal funds) that was paid to me during the period beginning with my first day of eligibility for SSI or the first day to which SSI benefits were reinstated after a period of suspension or termination and ending with the month that SSI payments actually began (or the following month if the local social services district cannot stop delivery of my last public assistance payment during the month that SSI payments began).

After taking this money from my SSI check(s), the local social services district will pay me the balance, if there is any, no later than 10 working days from the date it receives my SSI payment. I also understand that if the district takes more money than I believe was paid to me as Public Assistance, I will be given an opportunity for a hearing.

I understand that:
- the SSA may treat the date that I submit this signed authorization to the local social services district as the date I first become eligible for SSI if I submit an application for initial SSI benefits within the next 60 days.
- this authorization will apply to any SSI application or appeal which is presently pending before the SSA with respect to me and to any SSI application I make or appeal I request with respect to the period ending one year after I sign this agreement.

This authorization will terminate one (1) year after it is received by the local social service district and will not have any effect upon future SSI applications, appeals or reviews if my case is completely decided, if the SSA makes an initial payment of SSI either on my appplication or after a period of suspension or termination or if the State and I mutually agree to terminate the authorization.

CERTICATION - In signing this application, I swear and affirm that the information I have given or have been requested to give to the Department of Social Services as a basis for PA or care or for MA or for Services or for FS is true and correct. I understand that upon receipt of MA a claim may be filed against my property, after my death if I was 65 years or older when I received MA and at the time of my death I have no living spouse or children who are certfied blind, certified disabled, or under 21 years of age, I further understand that a recovery or adjustment may be made out of my estate, for any MA paid on my behalf while I am 65 years of age or older, If at the time of such recovery or adjustment I have no surviving spouse, and no surviving child who is under 21 years of age or is blind or permanently and totally disabled. I also understand that MA paid on my behalf may be recovered from persons having legal responsibility for my support at the time medical services are obtained.

APPLICANT/REPRESENTATIVE	DATE SIGNED	HUSBAND/ WIFE OR PROTECTIVE REPRESENTATIVE SIGNATURE	DATE SIGNED
X		X	

Fill Out the Application

The application for medicaid is a very long and difficult form to fill out. Using your own personal information, fill out as much of the form as you can. It is not necessary for you to fill out the sections of the form relating to other people who live with you. Just answer the questions that concern only you.

LESSON 16

Medical Insurance Claim

When you work for a company or join a union, you may receive certain benefits as an employee of the company or as a member of the union. One of the benefits is medical, or health, insurance. As an employee or a union member, you may have an amount of money deducted from your paycheck to pay for part of the insurance. The employer or union pays for the other part.

If you work for yourself, you may buy medical insurance directly from an insurance company.

Medical insurance usually pays a percentage of your medical costs, including doctor visits, medical tests, prescription drugs, hospitalization, and surgeon's fees. Medical insurance policies are not all the same, so the percentage that is covered differs from one policy to the next.

With most medical insurance policies, you alone may be covered or you and all the members of your immediate family (husband, wife, children) may be covered.

▶ Be Prepared

There are two parts to most medical insurance claim forms. You fill out one part, and the doctor fills out the other part. Whenever you make an appointment to see a doctor, have a medical test, or check into a hospital, you should fill out your part of the form before you go. And you should bring the form with you, since you may have to leave it at the doctor's office.

Some doctors bill the insurance company directly for the cost of your medical care. After they are paid by the insurance company, they send you a bill for the rest of the amount they are owed. This is because the insurance company pays a percentage, not the whole amount, of the bill.

In other cases, doctors will expect you to pay them directly for the cost of your medical care. Once you have made your payment, you send the claim form to the insurance company with both your part and the doctor's part filled out. The insurance company sends you a check for its percentage of the amount of the bill.

You should find out ahead of time which approach your doctor follows. This way, you can be prepared to pay him or her directly if necessary. You should also find out ahead of time how much the office visit or test will cost so that you can be prepared to pay with the correct amount of money. Sometimes, the doctor will send you a bill, so you do not have to pay when you are in the office.

On the claim form, you will be asked to provide information about the patient and the insured. The *patient* is the person being treated, and the *insured* is the person who has the insurance policy. The patient and the insured may be the same person. Or the patient may be someone covered by the policy of the insured.

You will need to provide very simple information about the patient and the insured, such as name, address, and employer. You will be expected to know your employee identification number, if you have one, and the insurance policy number. If you do not know the policy number, you can find out from your company personnel department, your union representative, or your insurance company.

Medical Insurance Claim Form Vocabulary

authorize Approve.

reverse Other side.

spouse Husband or wife.

How to Fill Out the Claim Form

The following hints will help you fill out the claim form. The numbers in the following list match the circled numbers on the form. Some parts of the form do not have circled numbers. You should be able to fill in these parts of the form without any special hints or explanation.

The top part of the form is supposed to be filled out by the "Insured." That is you. The section at the left is about the patient. The section at the right is about the insured. You should fill out both sections, even if the patient and the insured are the same person.

The bottom part of the form will be filled out by the doctor (the "Provider"). Do not write in the bottom part of the form.

1. Fill in the patient's date of birth all in numbers. For example, if the patient's birth date is October 15, 1952, you would write "10" in the Month box, "15" in the Day box, and "52" in the Year box.

2. If the patient is covered by medicare, check the Yes box. If not, check the No box. (Information is given on the back of the form for people who are covered by medicare.)

3. In this case, you are the insured. If you are also the patient, check the Self box. If the patient is your husband or wife, check the Spouse box. If the patient is one of your children, check the Child box. If the patient is someone else, check the Other box and write the relationship of the patient to you. The patient must be someone who is covered by your insurance.

LESSON 16   MEDICAL INSURANCE CLAIM   **73**

4. Write the patient's job title or the name of the company the patient works for. If the patient does not work (for example, if the patient is a child), write "NA" (not applicable).

5. Write the patient's telephone number. Place the area code between the parentheses.

6. This question concerns the reason the patient is going to see the doctor. If the reason is an injury received in one of the kinds of accidents listed on the form, check the box that applies. If the reason for the doctor visit is not an injury, check the two No boxes.

7. If you have an employee identification number, write it here. If not, write "N/A."

8. Write the number of your insurance policy.

9. Write the name of the company you work for.

10. If your mail is sent to someone else who holds it for you, write that person's name.

11. Sign your name here after you read the information on the back of the form, which is on page 78. Your signature here means that you are giving permission to the doctor to give information about your medical condition to the insurance company. Write the date all in numbers.

Fill Out the Claim Form

You have a bad case of the flu and decide to see your doctor about it. Use your own personal information to fill out the form. You are the patient and the insured. You do not have an employee identification number. Your medical insurance policy number is 609312.

MEDICAL INSURANCE CLAIM FORM

PLEASE READ INSTRUCTIONS ON THE BACK BEFORE COMPLETING THIS FORM

INFORMATION ABOUT THE PATIENT

1. PATIENT'S NAME (FIRST) (LAST)
2. SEX ☐ M ☐ F
3. BIRTHDATE — MONTH DAY YEAR
4. DOES PATIENT HAVE MEDICARE? ☐ YES ☐ NO
5. PATIENT'S RELATIONSHIP TO THE INSURED ☐ SELF ☐ SPOUSE ☐ CHILD ☐ OTHER (SPECIFY)
6. OCCUPATION OR EMPLOYER
7. PATIENT'S TELEPHONE NUMBER ( )
8. IS PATIENT A FULL-TIME STUDENT? ☐ YES ☐ NO — IF YES, NAME OF SCHOOL
9. IS CONDITION RELATED TO: ON THE JOB INJURY? ☐ YES ☐ NO   AUTO INJURY? ☐ YES ☐ NO
10. DOES PATIENT HAVE ANY OTHER HEALTH INSURANCE? ☐ YES ☐ NO
    IF YES, PLEASE GIVE THE INSURANCE COMPANY NAME, ADDRESS, AND THE POLICY NUMBER.

INFORMATION ABOUT THE INSURED

12. EMPLOYEE IDENTIFICATION NUMBER ►
13. INSURED'S NAME (FIRST) (LAST)
14. SEX ☐ M ☐ F
15. POLICY NUMBER
16. EMPLOYER
17. HOME ADDRESS (NO. AND STREET) — APT. NO.
18. CITY — STATE — ZIP CODE
19. IN CARE OF
11. I AUTHORIZE THE RELEASE OF INFORMATION AS DESCRIBED ON THE REVERSE SIDE OF THIS CLAIM FORM.
    PATIENT'S OR AUTHORIZED SIGNATURE — DATE SIGNED: MONTH DAY YEAR

---

20. PLACE THE SERVICE WAS RENDERED: ☐ HOSPITAL (IN-PATIENT) ☐ HOSPITAL (OUT-PATIENT) ☐ OFFICE ☐ HOME ☐ OTHER (SPECIFY) _____
21. DATE ADMITTED — MONTH DAY YEAR
22. DATE DISCHARGED — MONTH DAY YEAR
23. DATE OF ONSET — MONTH DAY YEAR
24. DATE FIRST CONSULTED FOR CONDITION — MONTH DAY YEAR
25. HAS PATIENT EVER HAD SAME OR SIMILAR SYMPTOMS? ☐ YES ☐ NO
26. EMERGENCY RELATED? ☐ YES ☐ NO
27. WAS SURGERY PERFORMED? ☐ YES ☐ NO
27A. IF YES, TYPE OF SURGERY
27B. DATE OF SURGERY — MONTH DAY YEAR
28. NAME AND ADDRESS OF THE FACILITY WHERE THE SERVICE WAS RENDERED
29. NAME AND ADDRESS OF THE REFERRING PHYSICIAN OR OTHER PROVIDER
30. DIAGOSIS OR NATURE OF ILLNESS. RELATE WRITTEN DIAGNOSIS TO PROCEDURE BY ENTERING LINE 1, 2, 3, OR ICD-9 CODE IN DIAGONSIS, COLUMN 37 BELOW.
    1.
    2.
    3.

31. PLACE	32. TYPE	33. PROCEDURE (HCFA/CPT4)	34. MOD	35. MOD	36. FULLY DESCRIBE PROCEDURES, MEDICAL SERVICES OR SUPPLIES FURNISHED FOR EACH DATE GIVEN (explain unusual circumstances)	37. DIAGNOSIS CODE (ICD-9)	38. DATES OF SERVICE FROM MONTH DAY YEAR TO MONTH DAY YEAR	39. DAYS OR UNITS	40. CHARGE

42. "I CERTIFY THAT THE CARE, SERVICES AND SUPPLIES ENTERED ON THIS FORM HAVE BEEN RENDERED TO THE PATIENT, AND THAT I AM ENTITLED TO REIMBURSEMENT OF THE CHARGES INDICATED."
43. MY FEE ☐ HAS BEEN PAID ☐ HAS NOT BEEN PAID
41. TOTAL CHARGES ►
44. PROVIDER'S TAX IDENTIFICATION NUMBER
45. TELEPHONE NUMBER ( )
46. PROVIDER'S NAME, ADDRESS AND ZIP CODE
PROVIDER'S SIGNATURE — DATE SIGNED: MONTH DAY YEAR
47. PROVIDER'S GOLDEN STATE NO.

GOLDEN STATE INSURANCE
P.O. BOX 198
SANTA MONICA, CA 90401

Front of medical insurance claim form.

LESSON 16   MEDICAL INSURANCE CLAIM   75

MEDICARE ELIGIBILITY INSTRUCTIONS

Patients over the age of 65 may be eligible for Medicare benefits **or** they may be covered by their own or their spouse's insurance. Please follow the steps below to determine your primary coverage and help us process this form correctly.

1. Is the patient over 65? ☐ Yes ☐ No
2. Is the patient actively employed? ☐ Yes ☐ No
3. If the patient is married, is the patient's spouse actively employed? ☐ Yes ☐ No

If the answer to question 1 is yes and the answer to questions 2 **and** 3 is no, then Medicare is the patient's primary health coverage. Submit your Medicare claim first. Once it has been processed by Medicare, please forward the Explanation of Medicare Benefits (EOMB) to us to determine if further benefits may be available under your Supplementary contract.

If the answer to question 1 is yes and the answer to **either** question 2 **or** 3 is yes, then Medicare may not be the patient's primary health coverage. The patient may hold primary coverage through a group where the patient or the patient's spouse is actively employed. In this case, the patient is TEFRA/DEFRA eligible. Please enter the insured group number if any, and employer name (see items 15 and 16 on front of form). Then, place an "X" after the Identification number on the top of the claim form (see item 12 on the front of form).

ORIGINAL BILL SUBMISSION INSTRUCTIONS

Bills must be **originals** (not photocopies) and must contain all the information needed to process the claim. When submitting original bills, first make sure that the bill includes:

- The physician's or provider's name and address.
- The patient's name and address.
- The insured's identification and/or policy number.
- The date of service (usually the date you saw the doctor or provider).
- The charges (the provider's fee) for **each** service.
- A detailed description of services. If this is a doctor's visit, the diagnosis or the name of the condition (for example, appendicitis, upper respiratory problem) must be included.

If you have coverage for medical prescriptions and you have a prescription drug bill, please make sure that the bill includes the following:

- The name of each drug.
- The quantity of each drug.
- The charge for each drug.
- The prescription number.

If you have a private duty nursing coverage bill, please make sure the bills submitted include the following:

- The doctor's written orders or authorization.
- The nurse's signature, professional title (LPN, RN), and license number.
- The place of service.
- The hours of duty worked (for example 8PM to 8AM).
- The total number of hours worked.

PATIENT'S SIGNATURE

The patient must sign the claim form, authorizing the release of information as described below. If the patient is a minor, the signature must be that of the patient's parent or legal guardian.

"I hereby authorize any physician, health care practitioner, hospital, clinic or other medical or medically-related facility to furnish any and all records pertaining to medical history, services rendered, or treatment given to me or my dependent for purposes of review, investigation or evaluation of this claim.

I also authorize Golden State, or its agents, to disclose to a hospital or health care service plan, self-insurer or an insurer, any such medical information obtained if such disclosure is necessary to allow the processing of any claim.

If my coverage is under a group contract held by my employer, an association, trust fund, union or similar entity, this authorization also permits disclosure to them for purposes of utilization review or financial audit.

This authorization shall become effective immediately upon execution and shall remain in effect for the duration of this claim or term of coverage of my insurance policy including a reasonable time thereafter, until its final consummation. This authorization shall be binding upon me, my heirs, executors or administrators."

PHYSICIAN OR SUPPLIER INFORMATION

See Item 31, Place Of Service Codes

- W — Inpatient — Hospital
- C — Outpatient — Hospital
- K — Doctor's Office
- H — Home
- A — Ambulatory Surgical Center
- L — Independent Laboratory
- I — Independent Clinic
- S — Extended Care Facility and Skilled Nursing Facility
- N — Nursing Home
- X — Other Location

See Item 32, Type Of Service Codes

- 1 — Surgery
- 2 — Assistant Surgeon
- 4 — Anesthesia (General)
- 5 — Radiology (Global)
- 6 — In Hospital Medical
- 7 — Other than Hospital
- 8 — Laboratory
- 9 — Consultation
- 0 — Medical Diagnostic Test

- A — Ambulance
- B — Biologicals
- C — Blood
- D — Professional Component
- P — Purchase
- R — Rental
- S — Supplies
- T — Technical Component
- U — Used Durable Medical Equipment

GOLDEN STATE INSURANCE
P.O. BOX 198
SANTA MONICA, CA 90401

Back of medical insurance claim form.

CHAPTER 4

POSTAL FORMS

When you want to send a letter to someone, you put a stamp on the envelope and drop it in the nearest mailbox. However, if you want to send a letter or package using one of the special services offered by the postal service, you have to fill out a form at the post office.

You can send a package or letter using express mail, which guarantees next-day delivery. You can insure something, so that if it is lost or damaged, you will be paid for its insured value. If you send something using registered or certified mail, you can ask for a **return receipt**. This means that you will be notified that your letter or package was received.

You can also get a postal money order at the post office.

LESSON 17

Receipt for Insured Mail

You may sometimes want to mail something that is worth money. For example, at Christmastime, many people send gifts through the mail. You can insure something valuable at the post office. When you want to insure something, you must fill out a **receipt for insured mail**. If your mail is insured and it is lost or damaged, you will be paid for the insured value of what you sent.

The amount you pay for the insurance depends on the value of the item you are mailing. Something worth $75 will cost less to insure than something worth $150.

You should save the receipt until you know that what you have mailed has been received and that it has not been damaged. You cannot claim your insurance money without the receipt.

▸ ## *Be Prepared*

When you use insured mail, you must be prepared to tell the postal clerk the value of what you are sending so that it can be insured for the right amount. You will also have to decide what kind of mail service to use and whether you want a return receipt (see Lesson 20).

Receipt for Insured Mail Vocabulary

domestic   Within the United States.

fragile   Easily broken, such as glass or pottery.

insurance coverage   The amount an item being mailed is insured for; the value of the item being mailed.

perishable   Liable to spoil or go bad, such as fruits or vegetables.

▸ ## *How to Fill Out a Receipt for Insured Mail*

FRONT

The postal worker will fill out most of this side of the form based on how you want what you are sending to be handled. The following hints will help you give the information needed on the form or answer the questions the postal worker will ask you. The numbers in the following list match the circled numbers on the form.

1. The postal worker will fill out this section of the form, using the address you have written on what you are sending.

2. The postal worker will fill in the amount of postage based on the mail service you want to use. For example, if you are mailing something to someone far away and want to send it airmail, you will be charged extra.

3. Write the amount of the insurance you want. This should be equal to the value of what you are sending. The postal worker will fill in the fee for the insurance.

4. If you are sending a package and you want it to receive special handling, the postal worker will write the amount it will cost here. **Special handling** means that the item is sent by registered or certified mail, for example.

If you are not sure whether you want special handling, ask the postal worker to explain the different kinds of handling and how much each costs.

5. **Special delivery** is a kind of mail service that is faster than regular mail. If you want this service, the postal worker will fill in the amount it will cost.

6. **Restricted delivery** means that what you are sending will be delivered only to the person named on the letter or package. The mail carrier will not leave it in the mailbox or give it to anyone else. If you want this service, the postal worker will fill in the amount this service will cost.

7. A **return receipt** is a form sent to you by the mail carrier once what you have sent has been delivered. This lets you know that your mail has been received by the person you sent it to. If you want this service, the postal worker will fill in the amount this service will cost.

8. If what you are sending is fragile, liquid, or perishable, check the appropriate box. If what you are sending is none of these things, do not write anything here.

9. The postal worker will write here the total amount for the insurance and the other postal services you have chosen.

10. The postal worker will stamp the receipt.

LESSON 17 RECEIPT FOR INSURED MAIL   **79**

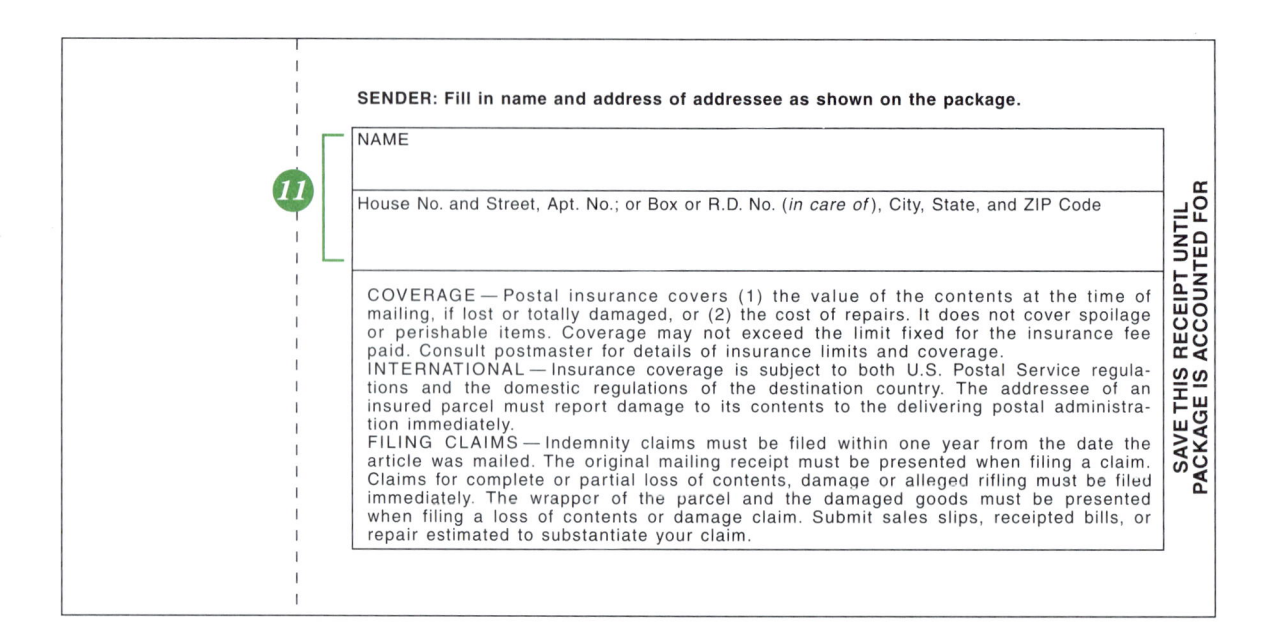

```
                    SENDER: Fill in name and address of addressee as shown on the package.
                   ┌─────────────────────────────────────────────────────────────────────┐
                   │ NAME                                                                │
          ⑪       │                                                                     │
                   ├─────────────────────────────────────────────────────────────────────┤
                   │ House No. and Street, Apt. No.; or Box or R.D. No. (in care of), City, State, and ZIP Code │
                   │                                                                     │
                   └─────────────────────────────────────────────────────────────────────┘

                    COVERAGE — Postal insurance covers (1) the value of the contents at the time of
                    mailing, if lost or totally damaged, or (2) the cost of repairs. It does not cover spoilage
                    or perishable items. Coverage may not exceed the limit fixed for the insurance fee
                    paid. Consult postmaster for details of insurance limits and coverage.
                    INTERNATIONAL — Insurance coverage is subject to both U.S. Postal Service regula-
                    tions and the domestic regulations of the destination country. The addressee of an
                    insured parcel must report damage to its contents to the delivering postal administra-
                    tion immediately.
                    FILING CLAIMS — Indemnity claims must be filed within one year from the date the
                    article was mailed. The original mailing receipt must be presented when filing a claim.
                    Claims for complete or partial loss of contents, damage or alleged rifling must be filed
                    immediately. The wrapper of the parcel and the damaged goods must be presented
                    when filing a loss of contents or damage claim. Submit sales slips, receipted bills, or
                    repair estimated to substantiate your claim.
```

BACK

11. Write the name and address of the person you are sending your mail to.

Fill Out the Receipt

You are sending your favorite niece a gold chain for her sixteenth birthday. The chain is worth $125. Her name and address are:

> Maria Delgado
> 1185 Fifth Street
> Columbus, OH 43212

Using your own personal information and the information above, fill out as much of the form as you can without having a postal worker with you to fill out the rest.

LESSON 18

Postal Money Order

If you do not have a checking account and you need to pay for something without using cash, you can get a money order from a post office or a bank. The money order in this lesson is a **postal money order**. A money order is like a check because it is used instead of cash to pay for things.

When you want a money order, you can go to the post office and ask a postal clerk for a money order in the exact amount you need. There will be a small charge for the money order. The postal clerk will print the amount on the money order, keep a copy, and give you the money order. The money order will be the top piece of paper. Underneath will be carbon paper and a copy of the money order. You should fill out the money order, detach the carbon paper and the copy, and save the copy. The copy is your record.

▸ Be Prepared

Before you go to the post office to get a money order, be sure you know the exact amount you need a money order for. For example, if you want to pay your electric bill with a money order, you can take the bill with you to the post office and read the amount you owe to the postal clerk. Or you can write down the amount you will need before you go to the post office. Be sure to double-check that you have written down the right amount.

You must have enough money to pay for the amount of the money order plus a small fee.

Postal Money Order Vocabulary

COD   Abbreviation for *collect on delivery*. For example, if you have ordered something that you will pay for when you receive it, you must have the right amount of cash or a money order worth the correct amount.

imprint   A mark made by pressure.

▸ How to Fill Out the Money Order

The following hints will help you fill out the money order. The numbers in the following list match the circled numbers on the money order.

LESSON 18   POSTAL MONEY ORDER   **81**

```
UNITED STATES POSTAL MONEY ORDER        15-800
                                         ———
                                          000

1   47797156866   921204   101281   ***23*95

    SERIAL NUMBER    YEAR, MONTH, DAY   POST OFFICE      U.S. DOLLARS AND CENTS

2  PAY TO                        5  CHECKWRITER        $$$$23 AND 95¢
                                    IMPRINT AREA

3  ADDRESS                       6  FROM

                                 7  ADDRESS

4  C O D NO. OR
   USED FOR

   ⑆00000800⑆:        47797156866⑈
```

1. This entire section is filled in by the post office, so do not write anything in this space.

2. Write the name of the person or company you are paying with the money order. For example, if you are paying your electric bill, write the full name of the electric company here.

3. Write the address of the person or company being paid.

4. If you are using the money order to pay for something being sent to you COD, write this information here. For example, you might write COD—TV set. Or, if you are paying a bill with the money order, write your account number here. Most bills have account numbers printed on them, so check your bill carefully to find the right number. If you are using the money order as a gift or for something that does not relate to bills or payments, you do not have to write anything in this space.

5. In this space, the amount of the money order was printed by the postal clerk. Do not write anything else in this section.

6. Write your name.

7. Write your full address.

Fill Out the Money Order

Suppose that you want to pay your telephone bill and have gotten a money order from the post office in the amount of $23.95. The name and address of the telephone company are:

> Orlando Communications
> 1275 Lake Drive
> Orlando, Florida 32819

Your account number is the same as your telephone number, including the area code. Even if you do not live in Orlando, fill out the money order.

82 CHAPTER 4 POSTAL FORMS

LESSON 19

Express Mail

The post office offers a special kind of mail service that delivers letters or packages overnight. This service is called **express mail**, and it costs more than regular first-class mail.

To send something by express mail, you must fill out a small form, which is then used as the address label for the letter or package you are sending. You can get the label at the post office. This form has two parts. The top part of the form explains what you must do to send something by express mail. It also explains what the post office will do to deliver express mail.

▲ Fold and Detach Stub Here ▲   IB736828103 US

Customer:
Please tear off this stub and keep it for reference when depositing prepaid Express Mail Next Day Service shipments in Express Mail collection boxes or when giving prepaid Express Mail Next Day Service shipments to Postal Service personnel. Affix the remaining label set to your shipment. DO NOT REMOVE THE CUSTOMER COPY. It will be completed and mailed back to you. For reference, write on this stub the date that shipment was mailed and initial the stub (if deposited in an Express Mail collection box). Deadlines for deposit for next day delivery differ according to the destination. To ensure next day delivery consult your local Express Mail Directory.

PRIVACY ACT: Your name and address may be used by the Postal Service to send you updated information about Express Mail service. You may request removal of your name and address from our mailing list by writing Assistant Postmaster General, Marketing Department, USPS, Washington, DC 20260-6300. Authority: 39 U.S.C. 401, 403, 404.

Additional information on Express Mail Service can be obtained at any post office or by writing USPC Headquarters, Washington, DC 20260-6334.

Date Mailed: **Initials:**

Service Guarantee:
If this shipment is mailed at designated USPS Express Mail service facilities on or before the specified deposit time for overnight delivery to the addressee, it will be delivered to the addressee or agent before noon or 3:00 p.m. the next day. Upon application by the mailer, USPC will refund the postage for this shipment if it is not delivered before noon or 3:00 p.m. of the next day, unless delivery was attempted, but could not be made, or because this shipment was delayed by strike or work stoppage. Consult your local Express Mail directory for morning and afternoon delivery areas. See The Domestic Mail Manual, Chapter 2, for details. Signature of the addressee, addressee's agent, or delivery employee is required upon delivery.
Express Mail International Service mailings are not covered by this service guarantee. See the International Mail Manual for details.

Insurance Coverage:
(See section 295 of the Domestic Mail Manual for exclusions of coverage such as negotiable items and consequential loss.)
(1) *Merchandise Insurance.* Merchandise is insured against loss, damage or rifling up to a maximum of $500. Idemnity will not be paid for spoilage of perishable items.
(2) *Document Reconstruction Insurance.* Non-negotiable documents are insured against loss, damage or rifling up to $50,000 per piece subject to a limit of $500,000 per occurrence.
(3) The maximum indemnity payable for negotiable items, cash, currency, or bullion is $15.

Claims:
• Claims for delay, loss, damage or rifling must be made within 90 days. Claim forms may be obtained and filed at any post office.
• The Customer Receipt must be presented when a claim is filed.

EXPRESS MAIL NEXT DAY SERVICE ®

Top part of express mail label.

This part of the form also has a place where you can write the date you sent the letter or package. You should tear off this part of the form and keep it until you know that what you have sent has been delivered. If your letter or package is not delivered on time or if it gets lost, bring this part of the form to the post office so that you can get your money back.

The second part of the form is the address label, which you must fill out. There are several copies of this part. One copy is pasted to the mail you are sending. You will fill out the label only once, because the extra copies are made when you fill in the top label.

▸ *Be Prepared*

When you go to the post office to send something by express mail, bring the name, address, and zip code of the person or company you are sending the mail to. Also bring the telephone number (including area code) of the person or company you are sending the mail to. In addition, you will need to write your own name and address, including zip code.

Be sure to bring enough money to pay for the postage. The lowest price for express mail is about $10. Anything that weighs more than a letter will cost more. This is because the cost of the express mail depends on the weight of what you are sending.

Suppose that you go to the post office for the company you work for in order to send something by express mail. Find out whether the company has an express mail account with the post office. Many businesses have accounts with the post office. If your company has an account, bring the account number with you and write it on the form. You will not need to pay for the postage, because the company's account will be charged.

Express mail is sent in special envelopes or packages. This means that you do not need to put whatever you are sending in an envelope. You will fill out an express mail label and give it to the postal clerk. The clerk will provide an envelope for your mail and will also attach the label to the envelope.

Express Mail Label Vocabulary

adhesive   A substance that is sticky.

to expose   To reveal.

indemnity   Protection against penalty or blame.

waiver   The act of giving up the right to or need for something.

▸ *How to Fill Out the Form*

The following hints will help you fill out the express mail label. The numbers in the following list match the circled numbers on the label.

1. If you are mailing something for your company and it has an express mail account with the post office, write the account number here.

2. If you work for a federal agency that has an account number for express mail, write the account number here.

3. If you are mailing something for yourself, write your name, address, and zip code here. If you are mailing something for the place where you work, put the correct person's name, name of the business, and company address and zip code here.

Express mail label.

4. When express mail is delivered, the person who receives it must sign a receipt stating that the mail was received. If you sign this section of the label, you are saying that it is OK for the mail carrier to deliver the package without getting a signature. The statement on this part of the label says that the mail carrier will leave the package in a safe place.

5. Write the name, address, and zip code of the person or company the mail is being sent to.

6. Write the telephone number, including the area code, of the person or company the mail is being sent to.

Fill Out the Form

You are working for the LifeLite Company at 436 Main Street, Tucson, Arizona 85726. Your boss, Mary Devlin, asks you to bring a package to the post office and have it sent by express mail. The package is to go to Lawrence Moore of the Sands Electronics Company, 95 Sixth Street, Minneapolis, Minnesota 55432. Mr. Moore's phone number is (612) 555-2360. LifeLite has an express mail account with the post office. The account number is 127-4398-2600.

Using this information, fill out the express mail label.

LESSON 20

Return Receipt

The post office has different kinds of special mail services you can use to send a letter or package. Some of the services are certified mail, registered mail, COD mail, and insured mail. When any of these services is used, the item being sent is given a special number, so that it can be traced if it is lost.

You can request a **return receipt** for any mail that is given a number. When you ask for a return receipt, a card is attached to the item. This card is mailed to you once the item has been delivered and someone has signed for it. This lets you know that your mail has been received.

All special mail services cost more than regular first-class mail. You must also pay extra for the return receipt.

▸ *Be Prepared*

When you ask for a return receipt, you need to have the name and full address of the person the mail is being sent to. You will also need to write your own name and complete address or the name and complete address of the person sending the mail if you go to the post office for someone else.

Return Receipt Vocabulary

addressee   The person or company mail is being sent to.

restricted   Limited.

reverse   Other side.

▸ *How to Fill Out the Receipt*

The following hints will help you fill out the return receipt. The numbers in the following list match the circled numbers on the receipt.

SIDE 1

1. You do not have to write anything on this part of the receipt. But you should read it carefully when you are in the post office. It has instructions for filling out the return receipt, what to do with the return receipt, and what to write on the mail you are sending.

SENDER:
- Complete items 1 and/or 2 for additional services.
- Complete items 3, and 4a & b.
- Print your name and address on the reverse of this form so that we can return this card to you.
- Attach this form to the front of the mailpiece, or on the back if space does not permit.
- Write "Return Receipt Requested" on the mailpeice below the article number.
- The Return Reciept will show to whom the article was delivered and the date delivered.

I also wish to receive the following services (for an extra fee):
1. ☐ Addressee's Address
2. ☐ Restricted Delivery

Consult postmaster for fee.

3. Article Addressed to:

4a. Article Number

4b. Service Type
☐ Registered   ☐ Insured
☐ Certified   ☐ COD
☐ Express Mail ☐ Return Receipt for Merchandise

7. Date of Delivery

5. Signature (Addressee)

8. Addressee's Address (Only if requested and fee is paid)

6. Signature (Agent)

PS Form **3811**, December 1991   ☆U.S. GPO: 1992—323-402   **DOMESTIC RETURN RECEIPT**

Side 1 of return receipt.

2. This section of the receipt asks whether you want other services with the return receipt. If you do, you must pay extra. The first service offered is item 1, which is the "addressee's address" service. This means that if the address of the person you are sending the mail to has been changed from the address you have, the post office will tell you the new address.

The other service is item 2, which is "restricted delivery." This means that the mail can be delivered only to the person it is addressed to. It cannot be delivered to anyone else, such as husband or wife, parent, child, neighbor, or coworker. If you want either of these services, check the correct box.

3. Write the name and address (including zip code) of the person or company you are sending the mail to.

4. Remember that the only kind of mail that can have a return receipt is mail that has been given a special number. Write the number here. The express mail label has a special number.

5. Check the kind of special mail service you want. In some cases, you might want more than one special service.

6. Sign your name.

7. The person who delivers the mail signs here, so you should not write in this space.

8. The postal carrier writes the date the mail was delivered here, so do not write in this space.

9. If you have requested the addressee's new address, the postal carrier will write it here, so you should not write in this space.

LESSON 20 RETURN RECEIPT   **87**

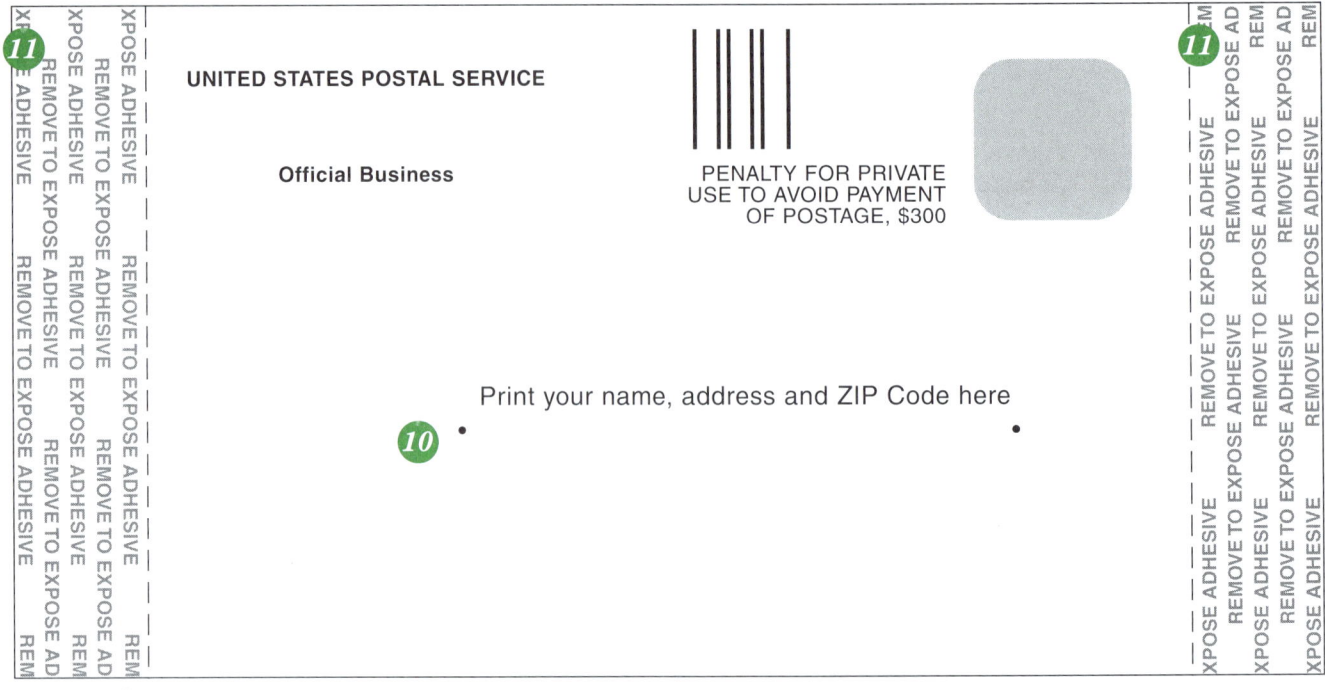

Side 2 of return receipt.

SIDE 2

10. Print your full name and address (including zip code).

11. Notice that two places on this side of the receipt have a circled number 11. Next to these numbers are strips with glue underneath them. When you have filled out both sides of the receipt, peel off the strips. Then press this side of the receipt onto the mail you are sending. It will stick to the letter or package. Later the postal carrier will tear off the signed receipt and mail it back to you.

Fill Out the Receipt

Suppose that you must send an important letter to your landlord, and you want to be sure that it is delivered. You decide to send the letter by certified mail, and you want a return receipt.

The landlord's name and address are:

Lennon Realty
135 Elm Street
Memphis, Tennessee 38150

The number for the certified mail is P 416 985 603. Use your own address even if you do not live in Tennessee. Decide whether you want the addressee's address and restricted delivery. Now fill out both sides of the receipt.

CHAPTER 5

CONSUMER FORMS

A **consumer** is anyone who buys or pays for goods or services from stores, businesses, or other people. You are a consumer when you buy a life insurance policy or rent a home or apartment. Every time you spend money, you are a consumer.

Many people use credit cards to make purchases. With a credit card, you sign a receipt at the time you buy something, and you are sent a bill later. Often, you do not have to pay the full amount you owe. Instead, you can pay in installments. There are different kinds of credit cards. Bank credit cards can be used in stores, hotels, restaurants, and many other places. Department store credit cards can be used only in the store that gives out the card. Gasoline credit cards are used to pay for gas by people who have cars or trucks.

LESSON 21

Bank Credit Card Application

Most department stores have credit cards. These cards can be used only in the department store that issues the card. Another kind of credit card, called a **bank credit card**, can be used in many different kinds of stores, such as clothing stores, drugstores, toy stores, hardware stores, and even department stores. In fact, some doctors accept payment with bank credit cards.

Many bank credit cards can be used throughout the United States and the world. You can get an application for a bank credit card in many stores and banks. Some applications even arrive in the mail.

If you decide that you want a bank credit card, you should find out which one offers the best deal for you. There are two important issues to consider. The first is the annual fee. Some cards charge an annual fee, which is an amount of money you must pay once a year whether you have bought anything or not. Other cards do not charge an annual fee.

The second important issue is the interest rate. If you charge something and pay for it a little at a time, you will have to pay interest on the amount of money you owe. The interest rate varies from one bank credit card to another. Try to find a bank credit card with a low interest rate, because the lower the interest rate, the less you pay.

There are other things to think about. Some cards offer special discounts on hotels and airlines. Others offer discounts on things they sell to you directly.

If you have never had a credit card, the first one is the hardest to get. This is because you do not have a credit history, which is also called a **credit rating**. Once you have a credit rating in one place, it is much easier to get other credit cards.

▶ Be Prepared

Banks want to know whether you are a good risk. They need to find out whether you are reliable and have the money to pay what you owe. This is why you will be asked questions about your work and personal finances. Be prepared to answer questions about your job and bank accounts or income you might have.

You should decide how you want your name to appear on the credit card. You may want your full first, middle, and last names to appear.

Or you may want your first and last names only, or you might decide to use your first name, middle initial, and last name.

Also think about whether you want other people to be able to use your credit card and how many cards you will need. Your wife or husband, children, and parents can use your card if you want them to. Each will receive his or her own card with his or her name on it. Since the credit card is yours, you will receive the bills for what they buy.

Bank Credit Card Application Vocabulary

eligibility   Meeting conditions for being accepted.

maiden name   A woman's last name before she was married.

self-employed   Earning money directly for yourself rather than wages or a salary from a company.

▶ ## *How to Fill Out the Application*

The following hints will help you fill out the application. The numbers in the following list match the circled numbers on the application. Some parts of the application do not have circled numbers. You should be able to fill in these parts of the form without any special hints or explanation.

1. "Apt. #" stands for *apartment number*. If you live in an apartment, fill in this section. If you do not, leave it blank.

2. This question asks how long you have lived at your present address. Write your answer in years. For example, if you have lived at your current address for seven years, write the number 7.

3. This section asks about whether you own a home or an apartment (condo or co-op), whether you rent a home or apartment, whether you live with your parents, or whether you have some other living arrangements. Check the box that fits your living arrangements.

4. Write your mother's first name and the last name she had before she was married.

5. In this section, write the name of the person to whom your phone bills are addressed. For example, your phone might be listed in your husband's or wife's name. If your phone is listed in your name, write your name in this section.

6. In this section, check off whether you are a permanent resident of the United States. It is not necessary to be a citizen to be a permanent resident.

7. Write the full address of the place you lived before you moved to where you live now. If you have always lived in the same place, you can write "none" in this section.

American BankCard

PRINT CLEARLY **PLEASE TELL US ABOUT YOURSELF**

| Print Your Full Name as It Will Appear on the Card (First, Middle, Last) | Home Address, Number, and Street | Apt. # | **1** |

| City | State | Zip Code | Years at Address **2** | ☐ Own Home ☐ Own Condo/Co-op ☐ Rent ☐ Live w/Parents ☐ Other **3** | Social Security Number |

| Date of Birth (Month/Day/Year) | Mother's Maiden Name **4** | Home Phone Number and Area Code ( ) | Name Home Phone Is Listed Under **5** | Are You a Permanent U.S. Resident? ☐ Yes ☐ No | **6** |

| Previous Home Address, Number and Street **7** | City | State | Zip Code | Years There |

| Employer **8** | Job Title **9** | Years at Job **10** | Business Phone Number and Area Code ( ) |

| Check Here if You Are: **11** ☐ Retired ☐ Self-Employed | If Retired or Self-Employed, Enter Bank Name **12** | Bank Phone Number and Area Code ( ) **13** | Bank Account Number | **14** |

| Total Personal Yearly Income $ **15** | Other Household Yearly Income $ **16** |

17 Other Yearly Income Sources

Check Those That Apply. Be Sure to Specify Bank Name.

☐ Money Market/NOW Account   Bank Name:
☐ Checking Account   Bank Name:
☐ Savings Account   Bank Name: **18**

☐ Visa/MasterCard ☐ Diners Club ☐ American Express
☐ Dept. Store/Sears ☐ Gasoline ☐ Other   **19**

20 If You Would Like an Additional Card(s)
Print the Full Name of the User(s) (First, Middle, Last)

PLEASE SIGN THIS AUTHORIZATION

BY SIGNING BELOW I authorize American Bank, N.A. to check my credit history and exchange information about how I handle my account with proper persons, affiliates, and credit bureaus if I am issued a card. I authorize my employer, my bank, and any other references listed above to release and/or verify information to American Bank, N.A. and its affiliates in order to determine my eligibility for the American Bank credit card and any future extension of credit. If I ask, I will be told whether or not consumer reports on me were requested and the names of the credit bureaus, with their addresses, that provided the reports. If I designate an authorized user, credit bureaus may receive and report account information in the authorized user's name. I certify that I am 18 years of age, or older, and that the information provided is accurate. I understand that if I use the card or authorize its use or do not cancel my account within 30 days after I receive the card, the American Bank Agreement sent to me with the card will be binding on me. I have read and understand the credit terms. **In order to be considered for an American BankCard you must complete and sign this application. Omission of any of the information requested in this application may be grounds for denial. Do not enclose a check for the annual membership fee. If approved, we will bill you.** Please allow 30 days to process your application.

X _____   _____
   Applicant's Signature   Date   **21**

Bank credit card application.

8. Write the name of the company where you work. If you are retired or self-employed, leave this part blank and see item 11 in this list.

9. Write the title of the job you have. For example, you might write "receptionist" or "clerk."

10. In this section, write the number of years you have worked for the company. If you have held a number of different jobs at the same company, write the total amount of time you have been there—in either years or months.

11. Check whether you are retired or self-employed.

12. If you are either retired or self-employed, write the name of the bank in which you keep your money.

13. In this section, write the phone number of the bank you named in item 12 in this list. The bank's phone number may be written on your **bank statement**, which is a record of all the banking you have done for a one-month period. Or check the phone book for the number.

14. Write the number of your bank account here. If you have more than one account (for example, savings and checking) at the same bank, try to fit both numbers in this space.

15. Write the total amount of money you earned last year. This is the amount before taxes were taken out of your salary.

16. If your husband or wife works, write the total amount of money he or she earned last year.

17. If you have any income in addition to your salary, write the total one-year amount here.

18. Check the boxes that apply to the kind of bank accounts you have. Then write the names of the banks.

19. Check whether you have any of the kinds of credit cards listed here.

20. Write the names of the people who will also have a credit card for this account.

21. You must sign this section of the application. It says that you give permission for the bank to check your credit history and references. It also gives permission for your references to give information about you to the bank.

Fill Out the Application

Review the application carefully and gather the financial information you need. Then fill out the form, using your own job and financial information.

LESSON 22

Department Store Credit Card Application

If you shop in department stores and would like to charge what you buy rather than pay cash, you can apply for department store credit cards. Many department stores accept some bank credit cards, but people often prefer to use a department store credit card.

Some department stores offer their charge account customers special sales or discounts. This is another reason to have a credit card from a department store.

As with bank credit cards, department store credit cards charge interest. The interest charged is a percentage of the amount of money you owe. You should find out what the interest rate is before you decide to open an account.

▶ Be Prepared

You can get a credit card application in the department store. Applications are often available throughout the store. You can take the application home, fill it out, and return it by mail.

The information needed to fill out a department store credit card application is similar to the information needed for a bank credit card application (Lesson 21). The department store will want to know about your job, income, bank accounts, and other credit cards.

Since you can fill out the application at home, you can gather the information you need at your own convenience.

Department Store Credit Card Application Vocabulary

authorize   Give permission.

consumer report   Information about a person's credit history.

inquiry   Request for information.

investigate   To look into or question.

obligation   Debt.

residence   The place where you live.

revealed   Let something be known.

subsequently   At a later time.

transactions   Business deals.

How to Fill Out a Department Store Credit Card Application

The following hints will help you fill out the application. The numbers in the following list match the circled numbers on the application. Some parts of the application do not have circled numbers. You should be able to fill in these parts of the application without any special hints or explanation.

FRONT

1. Write the information requested so that each letter or number you write fits within the tick marks.

2. If you have ever used a legal name other than the one you have now, write the other name here. This might apply to a woman who has changed her name through marriage or divorce.

3. Check whether you own or rent the place where you live.

4. If you neither rent nor own the place where you live, check the box and write an explanation of your living arrangements. This might apply to people who live with their parents, who are the owners or renters.

5. Write the number of years and months that you have lived at your current address. For example, if you have lived there for four years and three months, write "4" to the left of the slash and "3" to the right of the slash.

6. Write your birth date all in numbers. For example, if you were born on December 21, 1962, you would write "12/21/62."

7. Write the full address of the place where you lived before you moved to where you live now.

8. Write your job title.

9. The information wanted here is the total amount of money you earn in one year before taxes are taken out.

10. If you have been at your current job for less than two years, write the name and address of the place where you worked before you got your current job.

11. If you have any other credit cards, write the name of the company you got the card from. For example, if you have a MasterCard from a bank, write the name of the bank and then "MasterCard." Then write your account number.

12. This section of the form is about your banking. *CHK* stands for checking. *SAV* stands for savings. If you have a checking or savings account, check the correct box. Then write the name and address of the bank where you have the account.

CARROLL'S — APPLICATION FOR CREDIT CARD

1 NAME (FIRST) _____ (LAST) _____ HOME PHONE (INC. AREA CODE) _____
STREET _____ CITY & STATE _____ ZIP CODE _____ APT NO _____

2 PLEASE PRINT ANY OTHER LEGAL NAME IN WHICH YOUR CREDIT HAS BEEN ESTABLISHED _____ SOCIAL SECURITY NUMBER | | | | | | | |

3 PRESENT RESIDENCE INFORMATION
☐ OWN ☐ RENT **4** ☐ OTHER: _____   **5** TIME AT RES _____ YRS/MOS   **6** DATE OF BIRTH _____

7 PREVIOUS RESIDENCE
STREET _____ CITY, STATE _____ ZIP _____ YEARS THERE _____

PRESENT BUSINESS OR EMPLOYER _____ TYPE OF BUSINESS _____ BUS PHONE | | | | | | | | (AREA CODE)
BUSINESS ADDRESS _____ CITY, STATE _____ ZIP _____

8 POSITION _____   **9** EARNINGS/YR _____   YRS/MOS THERE _____

10 FORMER BUSINESS OR EMPLOYER (IF LESS THAN TWO YEARS AT PRESENT)
BUSINESS/EMPLOYER _____ BUS. ADD. _____ CITY, STATE _____ ZIP _____ YRS/MOS _____

DRIVERS LICENSE NO _____ STATE _____

11 OTHER CREDIT CARDS (DEPT. STORES, BANK CREDIT CARDS, OIL COMPANY)
COMPANY NAME _____ ACCOUNT NO _____

BANK ACCOUNTS
12 TYPE (CHK/SAV) BANK NAME _____ BRANCH ADDRESS _____

ALIMONY OR CHILD SUPPORT INCOME NEED NOT BE REVEALED IF YOU DO NOT WISH TO HAVE IT CONSIDERED AS A BASIS FOR REPAYING THIS OBLIGATION.

13 OTHER INCOME _____ SOURCE OF OTHER INCOME _____
14 PAYMENT TERMS ☐ OPTION (a) ☐ OPTION (b)

15 IF YOU WOULD LIKE ADDITIONAL CREDIT CARDS, WRITE THE FULL NAME(S) OF THE PERSON(S) TO RECEIVE THE CARD(S) AS THE NAME(S) WOULD APPEAR ON THE CARD(S). _____

16 I authorize Carroll's to investigate my credit history, and I understand that in connection with such investigation Carroll's may obtain a consumer report about me. Upon inquiry from me addressed to Carroll's Credit Department, Carroll's will inform me of whether or not a consumer report was requested. If such a report was requested, Carroll's will, in response to my inquiry, inform me of the name and address of the consumer reporting agency which provided the report. I further understand that if Carroll's establishes an account for me, Carroll's may subsequently, from time to time, obtain consumer reports in connection with transactions on my account. I authorize Carroll's to provide information concerning my account with Carroll's to credit reporting agencies and others who may properly receive such information.

I have read and understood the installment credit agreement. Signature _____ Date _____

Front of department store credit application.

13. For Other Income, write the total amount of money you receive other than your salary. If you receive child support or alimony payments, this money could be considered other income if you wish to include it. Then write where your additional income comes from.

14. This question is about how you will pay the amount of your bill. If you choose option (a), you are agreeing to pay your account in full each month. If you choose option (b), you can pay in installments. This means that you can pay a part of the bill each month. If you choose option (b), you will be charged interest on the part of the bill you have not paid.

15. If you would like other members of your family to receive credit cards and be able to use your charge account, write their names. Be sure to write their names the way they should appear on their cards.

16. Before a department store will give you a credit card, it will look into your financial situation and your credit history. Your

INSTALLMENT CREDIT AGREEMENT

In exchange for Carroll's extending credit to me, I agree that with respect to all purchases made by me or others authorized to use my account:

1. **Payment Terms. Option** (a): I may pay in full the new balance appearing on the periodic statement of my account not later than the next billing date shown on the statement (which shall not be less than 28 or more than 31 days after the closing date appearing on that statement) and avoid a **FINANCE CHARGE**; or, **OPTION** (b): I may pay each month one-tenth of my new balance rounded off to the nearer dollar. However, for balances under **$100,** the minimum will be **$10** or my new balance, whichever is less.

2. **Finance Charges.** If I choose **Option** (b), I will pay a **FINANCE CHARGE**, computed at a periodic rate of **1.65%** per month (an **ANNUAL PERCENTAGE RATE** of **19.8%**) on the average daily balance of my account (subject to a minimum charge of **50¢**).

3. **Receipt of Payments.** All payments required under this agreement shall be deemed to have been made when received by Carroll's.

4. **Defaults.** Carroll's may declare my entire outstanding balance to be due and payable if I default in making any required payment in full when due, and if my account is referred to an attorney for collection. I will pay an attorney's fee to the extent permitted by state law, and court costs.

5. **Changes in Terms of this Agreement.** Carroll's can at any time amend any of the terms of this agreement upon written notice to me.

6. **Limitation of Purchases.** Carroll's reserves the right to limit the extent of my purchases.

7. **Charge Card.** The charge card given by Carroll's to me shall remain the property of Carroll's and will be surrendered by me to Carroll's any time upon Carroll's request. If my charge card is lost or stolen, I will call Carroll's immediately or write to Carroll's.

Back of department store credit application.

signature gives the department store permission to find out about you. It also means that you have read the information on the back of the form and that you agree with everything stated there. Sign your name and write the date all in numbers.

BACK

You do not have to write anything on the back of the form. However, you should read the back carefully, since your signature on the front of the form means that you have read and understood the information on the back. The back of the form covers the following points:

1. This part is about whether you will pay your account in full each month or pay in installments.
2. If you pay in installments, you will pay a finance charge, which is interest on the unpaid part of your bill. The amount of the charge is explained.
3. Your payment is considered made when the department store receives your payment, not when you send it.
4. If you are late in your payments, the department store can request that the entire amount be paid in full.
5. The department store can change any of the items on this side of the form as long as you are told about the changes.
6. The department store can limit the amount of things you can buy with the credit card.
7. Even though the department store gives you the credit card, the card is the property of the department store. If the card is lost or stolen, you must tell the department store right away.

Fill Out the Application

Using your own personal information, fill out the application.

LESSON 23

Life Insurance Application

Life insurance is a kind of insurance that pays money to beneficiaries when the person who is insured dies. People who are the main source of income for their families often get life insurance so that the family will not be left without anything when they die.

Some companies offer life insurance policies as a benefit to their employees. Even if they have company life insurance, many people also get policies of their own.

The more money a policy is worth, the more you must pay. If you want to get life insurance, you should be sure that you can afford the policy. You will make the payments, which are called **premiums**, on a regular basis. Premiums are paid monthly or less often. You should discuss the amount of the policy and the specific kind of insurance you want with an insurance agent.

▶ *Be Prepared*

The life insurance agent will help you with the application. Therefore, you do not have to have answers to all the questions before you fill it out. However, you should have an idea of how much you can afford to pay. You should also know who your beneficiaries will be.

You will need the name and address of your doctor, or doctors, if you have more than one.

Life Insurance Application Vocabulary

beneficiary   The person who collects the money from an insurance policy when the insured person dies.

contingent beneficiary   The person who collects the money from the insurance policy if the beneficiary dies before the insured dies.

contingent owner   The person who will be the owner of the insurance policy if the owner dies.

owner   The person who has the insurance policy. The owner is often the insured person.

predeceased   Died before someone else.

proposed insured   The person applying for insurance.

revocable beneficiary   A beneficiary. **Revocable** means that the insured can change who the beneficiary is.

supplementary   Additional.

It is not possible to list here all the difficult or unfamiliar words that appear on the application. If you are not sure of what a word means, you can look in a dictionary or ask the insurance agent to help you.

How to Fill Out a Life Insurance Application

Some life insurance applications are very long. The one used for this book contains 16 pages. Only 4 pages are given here for you to fill out. They show the kinds of information you would usually find on most life insurance applications.

You will not be asked to fill out all sections of the form now. As mentioned above, an insurance agent will help you fill out the application. The agent will explain what different parts of the form mean. The agent will also be able to explain words or expressions you do not know. If you do not understand a question or some words in a questions, it will be OK to skip that question. The important thing is that you become familiar with the kinds of information you will be expected to provide.

The following hints will help you fill out the application. The numbers in the following list match the circled numbers on the application. Some parts of the application do not have circled numbers. You should be able to fill in these parts of the application without any special hints or explanation.

FIRST PAGE

1. Leave this blank.
2. Assume that you are the proposed insured. Write your full name.
3. Write "M" for male or "F" for female.
4. Your marital status can be single, married, divorced, separated, or widowed. Write the one that applies to you.
5. Write your birth date all in numbers. For example, if you were born on January 11, 1959, write "1/11/59."
6. Do not write anything here.
7. For feet, write '. For inches, write ". For example, if you are 5 feet, 8 inches tall, write 5' 8".
8. If you have other life insurance policies, write the total amount they are worth.
9. The insurance agent will explain to you the different kinds of insurance plans available. Do not write anything now.
10. The insurance agent will explain the different kinds of benefits available for the insurance policy you choose. Do not write anything now.

LESSON 23 LIFE INSURANCE APPLICATION

5537738-**3**

① ☐ Metropolitan Life Insurance Company ☐ Metropolitan Tower Life Insurance Company
☐ Metropolitan Insurance and Annuity Company ☐ MetLife Security Insurance Company

PART A — APPLICATION FOR LIFE INSURANCE

1. Identity of Proposed Insured

② Full Name   First, Middle Initial, Last Name   ③ Sex   ④ Marital Status   ⑤ Date of Birth Mo./Day/Yr.

State/Country of Birth   ⑥ Co. Use Enter Age Last Birthday   ⑦ Height Ft. In.   ⑧ Weight Pounds   Total Life Insurance in all companies (including Metropolitan)   Social Security Number

2. Address

Mailing Address of Proposed Insured, or Owner if named in Item 6. Number, Street, City or Town, State and Zip Code

3. Plan ⑨

(a.) PLAN (For VLI or FPMLI Complete Supplement II to Part A) $ (b.) AMOUNT (The Specified Face Amount or Guaranteed Insurance Amount)

(c.) COMPLETE FOR UNIVERSAL LIFE PLANS
   I. Death Benefits Option (check one)   (d.) For a qualified Plan Specify:
     ☐ Option A (specified Face Amount)   I. Type of Plan
     ☐ Option B (Specified Face Amount PLUS the   ☐ II. New Plan
        accumulation fund or cash value)   ☐ III. Existing Plan-
   II. Planned Premium Amount $ Employer Group No.

(e.) State any Special Request

4. Optional Benefits ⑩

☐ Disability Waiver   ☐ 1 Year Cost of Living   ☐ 10 Year Term $ ☐ Guarantee Issue: Option Amount
☐ Accidental Death   ☐ 1 Year Term $ ☐ 20 Year Family Income $ $

5. Premium Payments ⑪

(a.) Select a mode of payment which is available with the plan applied for:
   ☐ Annual   ☐ C-O-M   ☐ Govt. Allot.-Mil.   ☐ Govt. Allot.-Civ.   ☐ Sal. Sav.   ☐
(b.) Amount paid with application: $ ☐ None   This Amount ☐ is / ☐ is not at least equal to one C-O-M premium

6. Owner/Contingent Owner ⑫

(a.) Owner if other than Proposed Insured   Relationship to   Date of Birth   Social Security # or Tax I.D. #
    (Full Name of person or firm)   Proposed Insured

(b.) Contingent Owner (Full Name)   Relationship to   Date of Birth   Social Security # or Tax I.D. #
                                             Proposed Insured
(c.) ☐ Check here if Proposed Insured is to become the Owner if pre-deceased by both the Owner and Contingent Owner, if any, indicated above (only applicable if Proposed Insured is age 15 or over).

7. Beneficiary/Contingent Beneficiary

⑬ (a.) Revocable Beneficiary (Full Name)   Relationship to Proposed Insured   Date of Birth

⑭ (b.) Revocable Contingent Beneficiary (Full Name)   Relationship to Proposed Insured   Date of Birth

⑮ (c.) ☐ Check here if all present and future children born of the marriage of Proposed Insured and current spouse are to be included as contingent beneficiaries.

(d.) Address of Beneficiary or Contingent Beneficiary, if different from address in Item 2.

NOTE: (i) Unless indicated otherwise, if more than one beneficiary is alive when the insured dies, we will pay them in equal shares. If no beneficiary is alive when the insured dies, the contingent beneficiary will become the beneficiary. (ii) Any entry in Item 7 is invalid for a Corporate Pension or Profit-Sharing Plan or Public Employee Deferred Compensation Plan. (iii) A check in Item 7(c) above is valid only if the proposed insured's current spouse is named as the beneficiary.

Sample life insurance application—first page.

11. The insurance agent will explain the different ways that you can pay for the policy. Do not write anything now.

12. This section asks for information about the owner or the contingent owner of the policy. In this case, the owner is you, and you do not have a contingent owner. Do not write anything in this section.

13. You must decide who will receive the money from your life insurance policy. Write the beneficiary's name, date of birth (all in numbers), and social security number.

14. If the person you named in item 13 dies, the person you name here will become the beneficiary and receive the money from your life insurance policy.

15. Assume that your husband or wife is the beneficiary and your children are your contingent beneficiaries. If you want all the children from your marriage—even those not born yet—to be contingent beneficiaries, put a check mark in the box.

SECOND PAGE

16. If you are currently working, check the Yes box. If you are not, you should attach a letter to the application explaining why you are not working.

17. This section is about your use of tobacco. If you have ever smoked cigarettes, cigars, or pipes, write the last date that you smoked any of these. Smokeless tobacco is tobacco that is chewed. If you ever chewed tobacco, write the date for this. If you have never used any of these, check the Never box.

18. Write the reason you most recently went to see your doctor. Then write what the doctor said was wrong with you, what medicines or other treatments you were given, and the advice the doctor gave you.

19. Answer yes or no to questions a to f. If you answer yes to any question, fill out the section of the question called Details. If you answer yes to questions d or f, fill out the blank bottom part of the question.

THIRD PAGE

20. Answer yes or no to questions a to h. If you answer yes to questions a to f, explain your answers in the Details section. If you answer yes to question g or h, you will need a part of the application that is not included here. The insurance agent will provide you with this part.

21. If you have a driver's license, write your name in the first column, your license number in the second column, and the state that issued you the license in the third column.

5537738-**4**

8. Occupation

(a.) Occupation of Proposed Insured - Job Title and Duties

(b.) Employed by

⑯ (c.) Actively at Work? (If a homeworker, are you performing regular household duties; if a student, are you attending school regularly? If No, attach explanatory letter.)

How long?

Yes ☐ No ☐

9. Tobacco Use

⑰ Indicate date Proposed Insured last smoked/used:

cigarette	cigar	pipe	smokeless tobacco
☐ never	☐ never	☐ never	☐ never

10. Attending Physician

(a.) Name and address of personal physician, practitioner or health facility used by Proposed Insured

(b.) Date of last consultation

⑱ (c.) Reason for consultation and diagnosis, treatment and advice.

ITEMS 11. AND 12. APPLY TO AND ARE TO BE COMPLETED FOR ALL PERSONS TO BE INSURED.

11. Medical Data

For any Yes answers, give details below.
Has any person proposed for insurance:

(a.) In the last five years, been treated, examined, or advised by any physician, practitioner, or health facility? (Do not include colds, minor viruses or minor injuries which prevented normal activities for a period less than 5 days.) ☐ Yes ☐ No

(b.) Ever received treatment, attention, or advice from any physican, practitioner, or health facility for, or been told by any physician, practitioner, or health facility that such person had heart trouble, chest pain, high blood pressure, diabetes, lung disease, tumor, or cancer? ☐ Yes ☐ No

(c.) In the last two years, had persistent cough, pneumonia, chest discomfort, muscle weakness, unexplained weight loss of ten pounds or more, swollen glands, patches in mouth, visual disturbance or recurring diarrhea, fever, or infection? ☐ Yes ☐ No

(d.) In the last five years, received or applied for disability or hospitalization benefits from any source? ☐ Yes ☐ No

(e.) Ever had any surgical operation not revealed in previous questions or gone to a hospital, clinic, dispensary, or sanitarium for observation, examination, or treatment not revealed in previous questions? ☐ Yes ☐ No

(f.) Had a parent, brother, or sister with heart or coronary artery disease, high blood pressure, cancer or diabetes? (If Yes, give details for each person, including age at onset and age at death if applicable.) ☐ Yes ☐ No

Details

⑲

Item No.	Name of Person	Name and Address of Each Physician Practitioner and Health Facility	Dates and Durations	Nature and Severity of Condition, Frequency of Attacks, Specific Diagnosis and Treatment

Details for Yes answers to items (d.) and (f.)

Sample life insurance application—second page.

5537738-**5**

12. Non-Medical Data

For any Yes answers to Items (a.) through (f.), give details below.
Has any person proposed for insurance:

(a.) Ever had an application for Life or Health Insurance declined, postponed, rated, modified or required an extra premium? ☐ Yes ☐ No

(b.) Any other application for Life or Health Insurance now pending or planned in this or any other company? ☐ Yes ☐ No

(c.) Intentions in connection with the policy applied for, to borrow against, surrender or discontinue existing insurance or annuities (including Group) in force with this or any other insurer? ☐ Yes ☐ No

(d.) Had a driving license suspended or revoked in the last 3 years; or been convicted of 3 or more moving violations in the last 3 years; or ever been convicted of driving while impaired or intoxicated? ☐ Yes ☐ No

(e.) Been outside the U.S. or Canada in the past 2 years, or intend to be in the next 12 months? ☐ Yes ☐ No

(f.) Ever used heroin, cocaine, barbiturates or other drugs, except as prescribed by a physician or other licensed practitioner; or received treatment or advice from a physician or other practitioner regarding use of alcohol, or the use of drugs except for medical purposes, or received treatment or advice from an organization which assists those who have an alcohol or drug problem? ☐ Yes ☐ No

(g.) Flown as a pilot, student pilot, crew member or passenger (except on a scheduled airline) in the last 2 years or intend to do so in the next 12 months? If Yes, complete the Aviation Questionnaire. ☐ Yes ☐ No

(h.) Engaged in, or plan to engage in Automotive, Motorcycle or Power Boat Sports; Bobsledding; Ballooning; Scuba or Sky Diving; Hang Gliding (including Slope Soaring, Para-kiting, etc.); Mountian Climbing; Parachuting; Snowmobile Racing or any other hazardous sport or hobby? If Yes, complete the Avocation Questionnaire. ☐ Yes ☐ No

Details
Item No.

Driver's License Data

In ALL cases, give name, driver's license number and state of issue for each person to be insured.

Sample life insurance application—third page.

LESSON 23 LIFE INSURANCE APPLICATION **103**

FOURTH PAGE

22. If you do not have any other life insurance policies, you can go to the next question. If you have other life insurance policies, you must fill out this section of the form. Write your name in the first column, and write the name of the insurance company you got the policy from in the second column. In the remaining columns, write the amount of the policy, the kind of policy it is, and the year you bought the policy. If the policy is from the company you work for, put a check mark in the box at the right.

23. This section of the application is about your finances. Leave the top questions with the boxes blank. Your annual earned income is the amount of money you earn in one year before taxes or other deductions are taken out. The column at the right is for people who want more than $100,000 of insurance. At the bottom of this section, check the Proposed Insured box. This means that you will pay the premiums for your policy. You can leave the rest of the questions blank.

24. Write your current address in this section. You do not have to follow all the detailed instructions on the form in this case.

25. If you have changed your name within the last five years, write the name you had before you changed it.

Fill Out the Life Insurance Application

Using your own personal information, fill out as much as you can of the application. If you are not sure how to fill out some sections of the form, leave them blank.

5537738-**13**

SUPPLEMENTARY INFORMATION
(If Juvenile Policy, obtain information on Proposed Insured from Parent)

1. Details of Total Life Insurance In Force

Show all companies, including Group, U.S. Government, Fraternals, etc., for all persons to be insured

Name	Company (if Met., give policy number)	Amount	Plan	Year of Issue	Check if Bus. Ins.
					☐
					☐
					☐
					☐
					☐
					☐

Total Accidental Death Benefit in force on each person—give names and amounts, and indicate whether business or personal:

2. Financial Information

☐ Statement of Proposed Insured(s)   ☐ Sales Representative's estimate

	Annual Earned Income	Income from Other Sources Amount	Source	Personal Net Worth—complete for insurance amounts of $100,000 or more
Proposed Insured				
Spouse or Applicant for AWB				

Premiums will be paid by: ☐ Proposed Insured   ☐ Other—Name

Relationship to Proposed Insured   Estimated annual income of premium payer

3. Business Addresses

Print Proposed Insured's present and previous Business addresses. Give addresses for last 3 years if amount of insurance is $150,000 or less; for 5 years if $150,001 to $499,999; for 10 years if $500,000 or more. If more space is required, use Page 2.

	Employer	Street and Number	City or Town	State and Zip Code	From Mo. Yr.	To Mo. Yr.
Proposed Insured						
Spouse or Applicant for AWB						

4. Residence Addresses

Print Proposed Insured's present and previous Residence Addresses. Give addresses for last 3 years if amount of insurance is $150,000 or less; for 5 years if $150,001 to $499,999; for 10 years if $500,000 or more. Also give this information for others to be insured if different from Proposed Insured. If more space is required, use Page 2.

	Street and Number (If R.D., state number) Apt. No. or Floor	City or Town (If in country, give distance from and name of trading town and nearest post office.)	State and Zip Code	From Mo. Yr.	To Mo. Yr.
Proposed Insured					
Spouse or Applicant for AWB					

5. Previous Name

Give previous name for any change of name within last 5 years (applies to any person insured):

6. Telephone Numbers

	Number:	Most convenient time for call:	Most convenient place to call:
Proposed Insured:			
Spouse or Applicant for AWB			

Sample life insurance application—fourth page.

LESSON 23   LIFE INSURANCE APPLICATION   **105**

LESSON 24

Lease

When you rent a house or an apartment, you must sign a lease. A **lease** is a written, legal agreement between you and the landlord. A lease states how much the rent is and covers other issues of concern to you (the tenant) and the landlord. It is important that you not sign a lease until you read and understand it. If you do not understand some things, ask the landlord, the real estate agent, or a friend to explain them to you.

Leases are not forms that you fill out. They are usually printed forms. The landlord fills in the form and sometimes adds items.

This lesson is different from the others in this book. A list of some items you may find in a lease follows. Then, at the end of the lesson, a lease is shown. You are asked to answer questions about the lease.

▶ Items Covered in a Lease

All leases are different. Some are many pages long, and others are quite short. Some are written in difficult, legal language, and others are written in "plain English." Also, some items will always be included in a lease, and others will not. Here is a list of some items you may find in a lease. The wording used will differ from one lease to another.

1. *Identification of the landlord and tenant.* The name of the landlord and the tenant will always be stated in a lease.
2. *Apartment or house being rented.* The address of the place being rented will always appear in a lease.
3. *Lease dates.* A lease will state the amount of time a lease is good for. This is called the **term** of the lease. This may be one month, one year, or several years. Everything in the lease, such as rent, applies to the **full term**, or the amount of time the lease is good for.
4. *Use.* The way in which an apartment or house can be used may be stated in the lease. For example, a lease may state that the tenant can use the apartment only as a place to live, not as a business.
5. *Rent.* Leases will always state how much the rent will be. This section of a lease also states when the rent must be paid.
6. *Security.* In this case, the word *security* means that the tenant gives security to the landlord in the form of money, which is often a month's rent.
7. *Services.* The landlord states what services will be provided to the tenant and what services will not be provided.

8. *Repairs.* This section of a lease tells what the landlord will repair and what the tenant's responsibility is.
9. *Alterations.* A lease will often state what kinds of changes, such as changing the flooring, a tenant will be allowed to make.
10. *Fire, accidents, and so on.* If there is a fire or an accident, this section of the lease states what the landlord is responsible for fixing and what the tenant is responsible for.
11. *Landlord may enter.* According to many leases, the landlord is permitted to enter the apartment or home for several reasons, such as making repairs or showing the place to the next tenant.
12. *Sublease.* Leases will often state whether tenants may lease the home or apartment to someone else.
13. *Defaults.* If a tenant does not live up to the conditions in the lease, he or she is said to default. Leases will state how a tenant might default and what the landlord can do as a result of the default.
14. *End of term.* This section of the lease states what is expected of the tenant when the term of the lease ends.

Questions

First, carefully read the lease at the end of this lesson. Then, answer the following questions by writing your answers on the blank lines.

1. How much rent must the tenant pay in one month? _____
2. Is the tenant allowed to put up wallpaper without the landlord's permission? _____
3. Where does it state that the landlord will provide hot and cold water? (Write the heading where this can be found.)
   _____
4. Is the tenant renting a house or an apartment?
   _____
5. If the tenant breaks a chair, does the landlord have to fix it?
   _____
6. If the tenant puts in a new floor, who owns the floor?
   _____
7. Will the tenant get back the amount paid for security if she leaves the apartment in good condition?
   _____
8. How many years is the lease good for? _____

LEASE AGREEMENT

The Landlord and Tenant agree to lease the Apartment at the Rent and for the Term stated on these terms:

LANDLORD _Carly Meyer_ **TENANT** _Melinda Montooth_

Address for Notice _15 Adams Place_ _19 Jefferson Court_
Ruby Valley, Nevada 89833 _Wadsworth, Nevada 89444_

Apartment at _23 Decatur Blvd., Apt. 29, Wadsworth_

Lease date _January 1_ 19 _93_	Term _1 year_ beginning _January 1_ 19 _93_ ending _December 31_ 19 _93_	Monthly Rent $ _600.00_ Security $ _600.00_

1. USE: The Apartment must be used only as a private Apartment to live in and for no other reason. Only a party signing this lease and the spouse and children of that party may use the Apartment.

2. RENT: The rent payment for each month must be paid on the first day of that month at Landlord's address. Rent must be paid in full and no amount subtracted from it. The first month's rent is to be paid when Tenant signs this Lease.

3. SECURITY: Tenant has given Security to Landlord in the amount stated above. If Tenant fully complies with all of the terms of this Lease, Landlord will return the Security after the Term ends. If Tenant does not fully comply with the terms of this Lease, Landlord may use the Security to pay amounts owed by the Tenant including damages.

4. SERVICES: Landlord will supply: (a) heat as required by law, and (b) hot and cold water for bathroom and kitchen sink. Stopping or reducing of service(s) will not be reason for Tenant to stop paying rent. Damage to the equipment or appliances supplied by Landlord, caused by Tenant's act or neglect, may be repaired by Landlord at Tenant's expense. The repair cost will be added rent.

5. REPAIRS: Tenant must take good care of the Apartment and all equipment and fixtures in it. Tenant must, at Tenant's cost, make all repairs and replacements whenever the need results from Tenant's act or neglect. If Tenant fails to make needed repair or replacement, Landlord may do it. Landlord's expense will be added rent.

6. ALTERATIONS: Tenant must obtain Landlord's prior written consent to install any panelling, flooring, "built in" decorations, partitions, railings or make alterations or to paint or wallpaper the apartment. Tenant must not change the plumbing, ventilating, air conditioning, electric or heating systems. If consent is given, the alterations and installations shall become the property of Landlord when completed and paid for, and shall remain with and as part of the Apartment at the end of the Term. Landlord has the right to demand that Tenant remove the alterations and installations before the end of the Term. The demand shall be by notice, given at least 15 days before the end of the term. Landlord is not required to do or pay for any work unless stated in this Lease.

7. FIRE, ACCIDENT, DEFECTS, DAMAGE: Tenant must give Landlord prompt notice of fire, accident, damage or dangerous or defective condition. If the Apartment can not be used because of fire or other casualty, Tenant is not required to pay for the time the Apartment is unusable. Landlord need only repair the damaged structural parts of the Apartment. Landlord is not required to repair or replace any equipment, fixtures, furnishings or decorations unless originally installed by Landlord. Landlord is not responsible for delays due to settling insurance claims, obtaining estimates, labor and supply problems or any other cause not fully under Landlord's control.

8. LANDLORD MAY ENTER: Landlord may at reasonable times, enter the Apartment to examine, to make repairs or alterations, and to show it to possible buyers, lenders or tenants.

9. ASSIGNMENT AND SUBLEASE: Tenant must not assign this Lease or sublet all or part of the Apartment or permit any other person to use the Apartment. If Tenant does, Landlord has the right to cancel the Lease as stated in the Default section.

10. TENANT'S DEFAULTS AND LANDLORD'S REMEDIES:
A. Landlord may give 5 days written notice to Tenant to correct any of the following defaults:
1. Failure to pay rent or added rent on time.
2. Improper assignment of the Lease, improper subletting all or part of the Apartment.
3. Improper conduct by Tenant or other occupant of the Apartment.
4. Failure to fully perform any other term in the Lease.
B. If Tenant fails to correct the defaults in section A. within the 5 days, Landlord may cancel the Lease by giving Tenant a written 3 day notice stating the date the Term will end. On that date the Term and Tenant's rights in this Lease automatically end and Tenant must leave the Apartment and give Landlord the keys. Tenant continues to be responsible for rent, expenses, damages and losses.

11. END OF TERM: At the end of the Term, Tenant must: leave the Apartment clean and in good condition, subject to ordinary wear and tear; remove all of Tenant's property and all Tenant's installations and decorations; repair all damages to the Apartment and Building caused by moving; and restore the Apartment to its condition at the beginning of the Term.

Signatures: Landlord and Tenant have signed this Lease as of the date at the top.
LANDLORD: _Carly Meyer_ **TENANT:** _Melinda Montooth_
WITNESS _Jacinta Washington_

CHAPTER 6

GOVERNMENT FORMS

▲

Many of the important things you do in life require you to fill out a government form. For example, before you can work, you must apply for a social security card. Once you are working and earning money, you must fill out a tax return. If you want to get married, you must apply for a marriage license. If you want to drive, you must apply for a driver's license.

You cannot travel to a foreign country without a passport. And if you want to vote, you must first register by filling out a voter registration form.

In addition to the forms in this chapter, there are other government forms in this book. In Chapter 1, you filled out other government forms, such as the tax form (W-4). All postal forms are also government forms.

LESSON 25

Application for Driver's License

Everyone who drives must have a driver's license. Many states require that you get a learner's permit before you can get a driver's license. This gives you permission to learn how to drive and to practice driving before you take a driving test and get your license.

Be Prepared

Whether you apply for a learner's permit or driver's license, most states require that you provide proof of identity (you are who you say you are) and proof of age. There are many things you can use for proof of identity. For example, in this lesson, the application for a driver's license comes from New York State. New York provides a list of ways for you to prove your identity.

PROOF OF NAME

Please bring one or more of the documents listed below that add up to a total value of 6 or more. **Multiple documents of the same proof count as one proof.** At least one of them must have your signature on it. If the total value of your documents is less than 6, bring as many different proofs as you can (i.e. valid non-photo driver license, court papers for name change, government issued professional license). An office supervisor MAY approve them. For your own protection, we need to make sure you are who you say you are. Thanks for your cooperation.

DOCUMENT	VALUE
• NYS Photo Driver License	6
• NYS Photo Non-Driver ID	6
• IF UNDER AGE 21 — Affidavit by parent or legal guardian (See special instructions and requirements on Form MV-45)	6
• NYS Computer Generated Learner Permit	3
• U.S. Passport	3
• Foreign Passport— In English and with a U.S. VISA STAMP or I-94 attached. If not in English, a certified translation by the embassy or consulate of the issuing country or by an INS approved Refugee Resettlement Agency is required	3
• Citizenship or Naturalization Papers	3

DOCUMENT	VALUE
• Welfare/Medicaid Card (Must have your photo)	2
• NYS DMV Non-Photo Document (For example, a Vehicle Certificate of Title, Registration Receipt or Interim License)	2
• Pay Stub (Computer printed)	2
• High School ID With Report Card	2
• College ID With Photo and Transcript	2
• Marriage or Divorce Record	2
• Food Stamp Card (Must have your photo)	1
• Supermarket Check Cashing Card (Must have your signature)	1
• Parole Papers (Issued in arrest name)	1
• Cash Card (ATM) (Must have your signature)	1

Part of a list of documents to prove identity.

A value is assigned to each kind of identification. The identifications you have must add up to 6 before New York will accept your proof of identity. For proof of age, a birth certificate is usually required.

Application for Driver's License Vocabulary

convulsive disorder   Illness which causes uncontrollable physical fits.

expired   The time that something is good for has run out.

forfeited bail   Paid bail for breaking a traffic law and then did not show up in court. A person who forfeited bail did not get the bail money back.

revoked   Taken away.

traffic infraction   Breaking a traffic law, by going through a red light, and so on.

valid   Properly legal.

vehicle   Car, truck, or other form of transportation.

waived   Put aside or gave up the need for or right to something.

How to Fill Out the Form

The following hints will help you fill out the application for a driver's license. The numbers in the following list match the circled numbers on the application. Some parts of the application do not have circled numbers. You should be able to fill in these parts of the form without any special hints or explanation.

PAGE 1

1. Do not fill in this part of the form.
2. Print each of the letters of your name between each of the tick marks. Leave spaces between your last, first, and middle names.
3. Write your birth date all in numbers, like this: "12 11 65." Write each digit of each number between the tick marks.
4. *M* stands for "male," and *F* stands for "female." Put a check mark or an *X* in the right box.
5. Write each digit of each number of your social security number between the tick marks.
6. Use the two-letter abbreviation for the state in which you live. Put each letter between the tick marks.
7. If you are living somewhere temporarily, write your permanent address here. If your current mailing address is your permanent address, you do not have to write in this box.
8. A driver's license is accepted in many places as a form of identification. So, people who do not drive can get cards that they can use for identification only. These people must fill out the same application and provide the same information as people who do drive.

LESSON 25   APPLICATION FOR DRIVER'S LICENSE   **111**

New York State Department of Motor Vehicles

DRIVER'S LICENSE APPLICATION

PLEASE **PRINT** IN INK IN THE WHITE BOXES

1 Batch File No.

LRC   LAM   LRN   LDP   LNO   LIS

2 LAST NAME   FIRST NAME   MIDDLE NAME

3 DATE OF BIRTH: Month / Day / Year

4 SEX: M / F   HEIGHT: Ft. / Inches   EYE COLOR

5 SOCIAL SECURITY NUMBER

CURRENT MAILING ADDRESS (Include Street Number and Name, Rural Delivery, Box and/or Apartment Number)

CITY OR TOWN   **6** STATE   ZIP CODE   COUNTY

7 LEGAL ADDRESS (If different than mailing address)

Do you now have, or did you ever have: a New York State license? ☐ YES ☐ NO   or a non-driver I.D. Card? ☐ YES ☐ NO **8**

If "Yes", enter the identification number as it appears on the license or ID card.

ID NUMBER

9 Does any of the information on your license need to be changed? ☐ YES ☐ NO

ADDRESS CHANGE: CHECK THIS BOX. ☐ Complete form MV-232 (Address Change) if you have a vehicle registered in your name. **10**

NAME CHANGE: PRINT YOUR FORMER NAME EXACTLY AS IT APPEARS ON YOUR PRESENT LICENSE.

OTHER: WHAT IS THE CHANGE AND REASON FOR IT? (new license class, wrong date of birth, etc.) **11**

Do you have an out-of-state or Canadian license that is valid or that expired within the past year? ☐ YES ☐ NO **12**

If "Yes", where was it issued? _____   Date of Expiration: _____

Type of License _____   Driver's License No. _____

DO NOT WRITE BELOW--COMPLETE OTHER SIDE

Other Restrictions		OS	License Class	A	B	C	NCDL-C
				D	DJ	E	M	MJ
Endorsements			Special Conditions	AM	CS	DD	DP	LR	LS
Vehicle Restriction				ML	NF	UC	UP	UR

Expiration Date

Temporary License Endorsement

Proof Submitted
☐ Birth Certificate   ☐ Driver's License
☐ Major Credit Card   ☐ Passport
☐ Utility Bill   ☐ INS Papers

Other:

Validation Number

Approved by   Date

Office

MV 44 (9/91)

Page 1 of driver's license.

9. This application form can be used by people who already have a driver's license but need to change something on it. If you are one of these people, check the Yes box. If you are not, check the No box.

10. If you answered yes in item 9 and need to change your address on your license, check the box here. Notice that you must get another form, which you can request from the person who gave you the application.

11. Change of address and change of name are covered in special places on the form. This box allows you to write any other reason you might have for needing to change something on your driver's license.

12. You might have moved to your current address from another state or from Canada and had a driver's license from where you used to live. If you did, check the Yes box and answer the other questions.

PAGE 2

13. At the end of the first line of this section is a box where you must check yes or no. But you cannot answer yes or no until you have read and answered the rest of the questions that are part of question 1.

    This question is about illnesses or physical conditions that you might have. Put a check in each box that applies to you. Then go back and check the Yes or No box on the first line.

    Notice the note at the bottom of this question. If you answered yes to either of the first two questions, you have to get another form, which you and your doctor must fill out.

14. This question asks whether your driver's license was ever taken away from you or whether you have applied for a license before but had your application turned down.

15. The vocabulary for this lesson explains *traffic infraction* and *forfeited bail*. If you answer yes to this question, fill out the rest of the information.

16. This section of the form is for the parents of people who apply for a driver's license and are underage.

17. In item 12 on page 1 of the form, you were asked whether you had a driver's license from another state or from Canada. If you had a valid driver's license and have not failed a driving test in New York State, you can ask that you be given a driver's license without having to take a driving test.

18. This section of the form is for people who want a commercial driver's license, such as cab drivers or truck drivers.

13
1. Have you had, or are you being treated for, any of the following, or has a previous disability worsened? ☐ YES ☐ NO
   If "Yes", check all that apply.
   ☐ 1. Convulsive disorder, epilepsy, fainting or dizzy spells, or any condition which causes unconsciousness
   ☐ 2. Heart ailment
   ☐ 3. Hearing impairment
   ☐ 4. Lost use of leg, arm, foot, hand, or eye
   ☐ 5. Other (explain) _____
   If you checked box 1 or 2, obtain the appropriate medical form from a Motor Vehicle office. The form must be completed by you and your physician.

14
2. Have you had a driver's license, permit, or privilege to operate a motor vehicle suspended, revoked or cancelled, or an application for a license denied in this state or elsewhere? ☐ YES ☐ NO
   If "Yes", has your license, permit or privilege been restored or your application approved? ☐ YES ☐ NO

15
3. Have you been found guilty of a traffic infraction (except parking violations) or vehicle-related crime or offense, or forfeited bail in any such case in any court either in this state or elsewhere within the past 4 years? ☐ YES ☐ NO
   If "Yes", give details below. If more space is needed, attach an addditional sheet.

Date (*Mo/Day/Yr*)	Crime, Infraction, or Offense	Court & Location
/ /		
/ /		

16 **JUNIOR LICENSES** ☐ CONSENT: I am the parent or guardian of the applicant, and I consent to the issuance of a permit or license to him/her. *If the applicant is 17 years old and has a Driver Education "Blue Card" (Student's Certificate, Form MV-285), consent is not required.*

▶ _____
(Signature of Parent or Guardian)   (Relationship to Applicant)   (Date)

17 **ROAD TEST AND WRITTEN TEST WAIVER**
For holders of out-of-state or Canadian licenses, check box to request exemption from road test and written test.

☐ I request that the road test and written test be waived because I hold an out-of-state or Canadian license that is valid or that expired within the past year.

In signing the certification below, I certify that I was a permanent resident of the state or province in which the license was issued when it was issued, that THE LICENSE HAS BEEN IN EFFECT FOR AT LEAST 6 MONTHS, and that I have not failed a road test for a New York State driver license within the past 12 months. I understand that the waiver of the road test and written test is at the discretion of the Commissioner of Motor Vehicles.

18 If you are applying for a Commercial Driver's License and will be driving interstate, do you meet Federal 49 CFR Part 391 physical qualifications and medical requirements for driving in interstate commerce? ☐ YES ☐ NO

CERTIFICATION - I, the undersigned, state that the information I have given on this application is true to the best of my knowledge. If a duplicate license or record of convictions is being applied for, I certifiy that I am the holder of a valid New York State driver's license that is not presently suspended or revoked, and that this license or record of convictions has been lost, mutilated or destroyed. If I find the lost license after the duplicate license has been issued, I will turn it in to the Department of Motor Vehicles.

19 **SIGN HERE** ▶ _____
(Sign name in full - A married woman must use her own first name.)

IMPORTANT: Making a false statement in any license application or in any proof or statements in connection with it, or deceiving or substituting, or causing another to deceive or substitute in connection with such application, is a misdemeanor under Section 392 of the Vehicle and Traffic Law, and may also result in the revocation or suspension of your license pursuant to regulations established by the Commissioner.

20 **VOTER REGISTRATION** If you are not registered to vote at your current address you may receive a registration form here today. You may receive government services without being registered to vote. Would you like a registration form? ☐ YES ☐ NO

21 FOR OFFICE USE ONLY - TEST RESULTS   Applicant's Signature   Examiner's Initials

Eye	☐ pass	☐ corr lens	1	
1st Written	☐ pass	☐ fail	2	
2nd Written	☐ pass	☐ fail	3	
1st Road	☐ pass	☐ fail	4	
2nd Road	☐ pass	☐ fail	5	

MV-44 (9/91)

Page 2 of driver's license.

19. When you sign this section of the form, it means, in a sense, that you are swearing that the information you have provided in the form is true.

20. This part of the form does not relate to a driver's license. It states that, if you want to, you can receive a voter registration form when you hand in your application.

21. Do not write anything here.

Fill Out the Form

You can now fill out the form. Even if you do not live in New York State, it is OK to use your own address in this lesson. If you do not have a driver's license, you can fill out the form as if you were applying for one now. Answer only those questions that are about a new driver's license.

If you already have a driver's license, pretend that you have moved to New York State and are applying for a new one. If you do live in New York, pretend that you have just moved there.

LESSON 26

Application for Marriage License

Before you can get married, you must have a **marriage license**. Marriage licenses are handled by local governments and vary from city to city and county to county. Some places require that you wait a certain number of days after applying for the license before you can get married; other places do not. The number of days you have to wait also varies from place to place.

In some cases, you and the person you are planning to marry may be asked to take a blood test or other kinds of medical tests. You cannot get married until the results of the tests are in. For example, the marriage license in this lesson is from Detroit, Michigan. When you apply for the license, you are provided with several pages of information. One of the topics covered in this information is health requirements.

HEALTH CERTIFICATE: Beginning March 30, 1989, Marriage Applicants will be required by the State Law to receive counseling and be offered appropriate testing by a physician or local health officer (or designee) regarding the transmission and prevention of venereal diseases and HIV infection.

The Wayne County Clerk recommends that you have a State of Michigan Health Certificate when you apply. You must have the State of Michigan Health Certificate when picking up the license.

▶ Be Prepared

Because requirements for marriage licenses differ from place to place, it is not possible to know ahead of time exactly what information you will need. Usually, you will be asked for your mother's maiden name—her last name before she was ever married—proof of age (such as your birth certificate), and the date your divorce was final if you were married before. Do not start gathering this information until you are sure you need it.

Application for Marriage License Vocabulary

birthplace The city, state, and country where you were born.

residence The place where you live.

▸ How to Fill Out the Form

The following hints will help you fill out the application for a marriage license. The numbers in the following list match the circled numbers on the application. Some parts of the application do not have circled numbers. You should be able to fill in these parts of the form without any special hints or explanation.

1. For women, enter the name you had before you were ever married—your maiden name.

2. *Present age* refers to your age in years, such as 25 or 34. *Date of birth* refers to the month, day, and year you were born. This can be written out, like this:

    March 30, 1962

    Or it can be written all in numbers, like this:

    3/30/62

    Either way is OK.

3. In the place for residence number, put the number of the house or apartment building where you live.

MARRIAGE LICENSE INFORMATION
Please Print

MALE		FEMALE
_____	and	_____
FULL NAME OF MALE (First, Middle, Last)	①	FULL NAME OF FEMALE (First, Middle, Last)
		LAST NAME BEFORE FIRST MARRIED, IF DIFFERENT
② _____ _____	②	_____ _____
PRESENT AGE DATE OF BIRTH		PRESENT AGE DATE OF BIRTH
③ _____ _____	③	_____ _____
RESIDENCE NO. STREET		RESIDENCE NO. STREET
_____ _____ _____		_____ _____ _____
CITY STATE ZIP CODE		CITY STATE ZIP CODE
④ _____ ⑤ _____	④ ⑤	_____ _____
RESIDENCE COUNTY TIMES PREVIOUSLY MARRIED		RESIDENCE COUNTY TIMES PREVIOUSLY MARRIED
⑥ _____	⑥	_____
BIRTHPLACE – CITY AND STATE		BIRTHPLACE – CITY AND STATE
⑦ _____	⑦	_____
FATHER'S FULL NAME		FATHER'S FULL NAME
⑧ _____	⑧	_____
MOTHER'S FULL NAME BEFORE 1ST MARRIED		MOTHER'S FULL NAME BEFORE 1ST MARRIED
⑨ _____ _____	⑨	_____ _____
FATHER'S BIRTHPLACE MOTHER'S BIRTHPLACE		FATHER'S BIRTHPLACE MOTHER'S BIRTHPLACE

WEDDING DATE: _____

**MARRIAGE LICENSE
GOOD FOR 33 DAYS ONLY
FROM DATE OF APPLICATION**

4. A county and a city are not the same. Most of the time, there are several cities in a county. If you are not sure of the name of the county where you live, look through the papers you received with the application. The name of the county will probably be printed somewhere on them. The name of the county for Detroit (the place where the application in this lesson comes from) is Wayne County.

Be sure that you read carefully so that you do not mistake the word *county* for the word *country*.

5. If you have been married before, write here how many times you have been married. Do not include the marriage you are now planning.

6. Write here the city and state where you were born. If you were not born in the United States, write the city and country where you were born, even though it does not ask for this information on the form.

7. Write your father's first, middle, and last names here.

8. Write your mother's first, middle, and maiden names here.

9. Fill in the city and state where each of your parents was born. If either or both of them were born outside the United States, write the city and country. If you are not sure of this information and cannot find out, write "unknown" on the form.

Filling Out the Form

Even though you may already be married or have no plans to get married, fill out your half of the application for a marriage license. This will be a good chance for you to gather the information that is required on the form, since you may need it in the future for a marriage license or some other form.

LESSON 27

Application for Social Security Card

Even though a social security card is very small, it is one of the most important documents you ever will have. Your social security card has a number on it. This number is yours for your whole life, even if you change your name. No one else has the same number.

When you are working, you and your employer pay money into your social security account. When you retire or if you become ill or disabled, you will receive regular payments, which are called **social security benefits**.

You are often asked for your social security number, even when you are dealing with something that has nothing to do directly with social security benefits. For example, many of the forms in this book ask for your social security number. These include applications for a passport, driver's license, school, job, and credit card. One reason for this is that you are the only person with your social security number. Identifying people by their social security numbers means that there is no confusion even when two people have the same name.

▶ *Be Prepared*

If you are applying for a social security card for the first time, you must go to your local social security office. You will need to bring documents so that you can identify yourself. These documents can include your birth certificate and one other document, such as the following:

- A driver's license
- A passport
- A school identification card, record, or report card
- A federal or state government identification card
- A marriage or divorce record
- A health insurance card
- Clinic, doctor, or hospital records
- Military records

The social security office will not accept ordinary copies of documents. You must have the original document or a certified copy. A **certified copy** is a special copy issued by a county clerk or other official who is in charge of records.

If you were not born in the United States but were born as a U.S. citizen somewhere else, you need to have the consular report of birth or a foreign birth certificate. If you are a naturalized citizen, you need to have a certificate of citizenship or certificate of naturalization. In either case, you may also use your passport for identification.

If you are not a citizen of the United States, you may still apply for a social security card. You need to bring a birth certificate or passport and any documents given to you by the Immigration and Naturalization Service, such as your alien registration receipt card.

When you fill out the application, you must know your mother's maiden name. If you do not know it, be sure to find it out before you go to the social security office.

Social Security Card Application Vocabulary

adoptive parents   People who take care of a child not born to them, raise the child as their own, and give the child their name.

ethnic   Relating to the racial, national, or religious background of a group of people.

legal guardian   A person who has legally been given the care of another, usually a child.

maiden name   A woman's last name before she was married.

previously   Earlier in time.

voluntary   Being free to choose.

▶ *How to Fill Out the Application*

The following hints will help you fill out the application. The numbers in the following list match the circled numbers on the application. Some parts of the application do not have circled numbers. You should be able to fill in these parts of the application without any special hints or explanation.

1. The name you have now may not be the same as it was when you were born. For example, your name could have changed when you were married. Write the full name you had when you were born.

2. Some people use a name that is not their real name. An actor may use a stage name but still keep his or her original name legally.

In other cases, a person may use a name in business that is not his or her name. For example, a woman named Ellen Kinski may own a beauty salon called Ellen Kay's Beauty Salon. For business reasons, she calls herself Ellen Kay. This woman would write her legal full name on the first line of the application. Then she would write "Ellen Kay" on the third line.

SOCIAL SECURITY ADMINISTRATION
Application for a Social Security Card

INSTRUCTIONS
- Please read "How To Complete This Form" on page 2.
- Print or type using black or blue ink. DO NOT USE PENCIL.
- After you complete this form, take or mail it along with the required documents to your nearest Social Security office.
- If you are completing this form for someone else, answer the questions as they apply to the person. Then, sign your name in question 16.

1 NAME To Be Shown On Card — FIRST / FULL MIDDLE NAME / LAST

FULL NAME AT BIRTH IF OTHER THAN ABOVE — FIRST / FULL MIDDLE NAME / LAST

OTHER NAMES USED

2 MAILING ADDRESS Do Not Abbreviate — STREET ADDRESS, APT. NO., PO BOX, RURAL ROUTE NO.

CITY / STATE / ZIP CODE

3 CITIZENSHIP (Check One)
- [ ] U.S. Citizen
- [ ] Legal Alien Allowed To Work
- [ ] Legal Alien Not Allowed To Work
- [ ] Foreign Student Allowed Restricted Employment
- [ ] Conditionally Legalized Alien Allowed To Work
- [ ] Other (See Instructions On Page 2)

4 SEX
- [ ] Male
- [ ] Female

5 RACE/ETHNIC DESCRIPTION (Check One Only—Voluntary)
- [ ] Asian, Asian-American Or Pacific Islander
- [ ] Hispanic
- [ ] Black (Not Hispanic)
- [ ] North American Indian Or Alaskan Native
- [ ] White (Not Hispanic)

6 DATE OF BIRTH — MONTH DAY YEAR

7 PLACE OF BIRTH (Do Not Abbreviate) — CITY / STATE OR FOREIGN COUNTRY / FCI — Office Use Only

8 MOTHER'S MAIDEN NAME — FIRST / FULL MIDDLE NAME / LAST NAME AT HER BIRTH

9 FATHER'S NAME — FIRST / FULL MIDDLE NAME / LAST NAME

10 Has the person in item 1 ever received a Social Security number before?
- [ ] Yes (if "yes", answer questions 11-13.)
- [ ] No (If "no", go on to question 14.)
- [ ] Don't Know (If "don't know", go on to question 14.)

11 Enter the Social Security number previously assigned to the person listed in item 1.

☐☐☐ – ☐☐ – ☐☐☐☐

12 Enter the name shown on the most recent Social Security card issued for the person listed in item 1.

FIRST / MIDDLE / LAST

13 Enter any different date of birth if used on an earlier application for a card. — MONTH DAY YEAR

14 TODAY'S DATE ▶ MONTH DAY YEAR

15 DAYTIME PHONE NUMBER ▶ ( ) AREA CODE

DELIBERATELY FURNISHING (OR CAUSING TO BE FURNISHED) FALSE INFORMATION ON THIS APPLICATION IS A CRIME PUNISHABLE BY FINE OR IMPRISONMENT, OR BOTH.

16 YOUR SIGNATURE ▶

17 YOUR RELATIONSHIP TO THE PERSON IN ITEM 1 IS:
- [ ] Self
- [ ] Natural Or Adoptive Parent
- [ ] Legal Guardian
- [ ] Other (Specify)

DO NOT WRITE BELOW THIS LINE (FOR SSA USE ONLY)

NPN			DOC	NTI	CAN		ITV
PBC	EVI	EVA	EVC	PRA	NWR	DNR	UNIT

EVIDENCE SUBMITTED

SIGNATURE AND TITLE OF EMPLOYEE(S) REVIEWING EVIDENCE AND/OR CONDUCTING INTERVIEW

DATE

DATE

LESSON 27 APPLICATION FOR SOCIAL SECURITY CARD

You are not being asked to give a nickname on the form. If you use another name for a special reason like the ones just described, write your name the way Ellen Kinski would.

3. Write the address to which your mail is sent. If you use a post office box for all your mail, write the box number and all the other information requested to complete the address.

4. If you check Other for citizenship, you must attach a statement explaining the situation and why you need a social security number.

5. The Social Security Administration uses race and ethnic information to study how social security programs affect different groups of people. People's names are not used in these studies. You can decide whether you want to answer this question. If you choose not to answer, do not write anything.

6. The item 1 here refers to the item 1 printed on the form, the place where you wrote your name. If you or the person you are filling out the application for has had a social security card before, check the Yes box and answer questions 11 to 13. If you or the person you are filling out the form for has never had a social security card, check the No box. Then skip questions 11 to 13 and go directly to question 14. If you check the Don't Know box, skip questions 11 to 13 and go directly to question 14.

7. If the date of birth on another application for a social security card was different from the date of birth given on this application, write the other date of birth here. You may write the date of birth in words (March 24, 1948) or all in numbers (3 24 48).

8. Write today's date all in numbers.

9. Write the telephone number at which you can be reached during normal working hours—9 a.m. to 5 p.m.

10. If you are filling out the application for yourself, check the Self box. If you are filling it out for someone else, check the box that applies. Do not write anything below this line on the form.

Fill Out the Application for a Social Security Card

Even if you already have a social security card, fill out the application for yourself, using your own personal information.

LESSON 28

Application for Passport

When you travel outside the United States, you often need a **passport** to enter a foreign country and reenter the United States. Passports are issued by the U.S. Department of State. To get a passport, usually you must go to a local passport office and fill out an application.

Some countries, such as Canada, do not require a U.S. citizen to have a passport to enter. You can visit these countries if you can prove that you are a U.S. citizen. On the other hand, to visit some countries, you must have both a passport and a visa. A **visa** is official approval by a country that you are allowed to enter that country. Visas are issued by the country you wish to visit.

In addition to visas, some countries have health requirements you must meet before you can visit them.

When you apply for a passport, you can get information about visas and health requirements from the passport office.

▸ Be Prepared

If you are applying for a passport for the first time, you must apply in person. You should be prepared to supply a number of things. The four most important are proof of citizenship, proof of identity, a photograph, and payment of the passport fee. In addition, there is certain information you must have available.

Proof of Citizenship   The passport office will accept a previous passport or a certified birth certificate as proof that you are a U.S. citizen.

If you have never had a passport and there is no official record of your birth, you must submit an official notice saying that no birth record exists. In addition, you must also have any one of the following items: infant baptismal record; hospital birth record; census, school, or family Bible records; newspaper files; or insurance files. You may also provide written statements from people who have knowledge of your birth. These statements must be **notarized** (stamped with the seal of a notary public—a public official).

If you were not born in the United States, you must have one of the these items: a previous passport, a certificate of naturalization, a certificate of citizenship, or a report of birth abroad.

Proof of Identity

The items you submit to prove your identity must have both your signature and a physical description of you. These items might include a previous passport, a certificate of naturalization or citizenship, a driver's license, or a government identification card. If you do not have any these things, someone who is a U.S. citizen and who has known you for at least two years must come with you to the passport office to prove your identity.

Photograph

You will need two copies of the same photograph. The picture should be 2 by 2 inches and must show your face only. In the picture, you should be facing the front. Very often, there are photography shops near passport offices that will take inexpensive photographs that meet the passport requirement exactly.

Passport Fee

A passport costs $65. The passport fee is $55, and the charge for handling the application is $10. The passport office will accept checks and money orders.

Things You Need to Know

In addition to the four important items just discussed, you will also need to know your mother's maiden name and the birthplace and birth date for both your parents. If you do not know this information by heart, make a note of it and bring it with you. If you do not know and cannot find out some or all of this information, write "Unknown" on the application.

If you are a married woman, you will have to know your husband's place of birth. If you are a married man, you will have to know your wife's maiden name and her place of birth. If you are widowed or divorced, you will need to supply the exact date of your spouse's death or the date the divorce was final.

Passport Application Vocabulary

administration   Giving.

departure   The act of leaving.

disposition   In this case, what happened to a passport.

maiden name   A woman's last name before she was married.

mandatory   Required or necessary.

province   A part of a country.

resided   Lived.

▶ ## How to Fill Out the Application

The following hints will help you fill out the application. The numbers in the following list match the circled numbers on the application. Some

124   CHAPTER 6   GOVERNMENT FORMS

parts of the application do not have circled numbers. You should be able to fill in these parts of the application without any special hints or explanation.

1. Check the box for passport.

2. Write the address to which your mail is sent. This does not have to be the place where you live.

3. You may live with someone whose name is registered with the post office and appears alone on your mailbox. In this case, the postal carrier may not know that you are living at this address. In order for you to receive your mail, it must be sent to you in care of this other person. If this situation applies to you, write the name of the other person here. If this situation does not apply to you, do not write anything here.

4. The information in this part of the form is provided by the people at the passport office. Do not write anything here.

5. Write the city, state, and country in which you were born. If you were not born in the United States, write the city and country.

6. Write your date of birth all in numbers. For example, if you were born on April 13, 1975, write "04 13 75." Put a number in each box. However, if the month or day of your birthday is only one number, as in April (4), write the number in the right-hand box for the month or day, and write a zero in the left-hand box.

7. Write each of the numbers in your social security number between the tick marks. Be sure to start at the left of the first tick mark so that the number will fit correctly in the spaces provided. If you do not have a social security number, write zeros in this space to show that you do not have a number, or leave this blank.

At this place on the form, there is a statement about the tax law. This means that people applying for passports must provide their name, mailing address, date of birth, and social security number on the passport application. The passport service gives this information to the Internal Revenue Service (IRS).

8. Write your hair color. If you dye your hair, the present color of your hair and your hair color in the photograph you supply should be the same. This is the color you should write in this box.

9. Your mailing address was requested earlier on the form. Write your permanent address here, even if it is the same as your mailing address.

10. Write your job title.

11. Write your father's full name, the country where he was born, and the month, day, and year he was born (all in numbers). Also check whether or not he is a U.S. citizen. If you do not

UNITED STATES DEPARTMENT OF STATE
APPLICATION FOR ☐ PASSPORT ☐ REGISTRATION
SEE INSTRUCTIONS—TYPE OR PRINT IN INK IN WHITE AREAS

1. NAME FIRST NAME / MIDDLE NAME / LAST NAME

2. MAILING ADDRESS STREET / CITY, STATE, ZIP CODE / COUNTRY / IN CARE OF

☐ 5 Yr. ☐ 10 Yr. Issue Date _____
R D O DP
End. # _____ Exp. _____

3. SEX Male Female

4. PLACE OF BIRTH City, State or Province, Country

5. DATE OF BIRTH Mo. Day Year

6. SEE FEDERAL TAX LAW NOTICE ON REVERSE SIDE SOCIAL SECURITY NUMBER

7. HEIGHT Feet Inches

8. COLOR OF HAIR

9. COLOR OF EYES

10. (Area Code) HOME PHONE

11. (Area Code) BUSINESS PHONE

12. PERMANENT ADDRESS (Street, City, State, ZIP Code)

13. OCCUPATION

14. FATHER'S NAME / BIRTHPLACE / BIRTH DATE / U.S. CITIZEN ☐ YES ☐ NO

15. MOTHER'S MAIDEN NAME / BIRTHPLACE / BIRTH DATE / U.S. CITIZEN ☐ YES ☐ NO

16. TRAVEL PLANS (Not Mandatory) COUNTRIES / DEPARTURE DATE / LENGTH OF STAY

17. HAVE YOU EVER BEEN ISSUED A U.S. PASSPORT? YES NO IF YES, SUBMIT PASSPORT IF AVAILABLE. ☐ Submitted
IF UNABLE TO SUBMIT MOST RECENT PASSPORT, STATE ITS DISPOSITION: COMPLETE NEXT LINE
NAME IN WHICH ISSUED / PASSPORT NUMBER / ISSUE DATE (Mo., Day, Yr.) / DISPOSITION

SUBMIT TWO RECENT IDENTICAL PHOTOS
2" X 2"
FROM 1" TO 1-3/8"

18. HAVE YOU EVER BEEN MARRIED? YES NO DATE OF MOST RECENT MARRIAGE Mo. Day Year
WIDOWED/DIVORCED? YES NO IF YES, GIVE DATE Mo. Day Year
SPOUSE'S FULL BIRTH NAME / SPOUSE'S BIRTHPLACE

19. IN CASE OF EMERGENCY, NOTIFY (Person Not Traveling With You) RELATIONSHIP
(Not Mandatory) FULL NAME
ADDRESS (Area Code) PHONE NUMBER

20. TO BE COMPLETED BY AN APPLICANT WHO BECAME A CITIZEN THROUGH NATURALIZATION
I IMMIGRATED TO THE U.S. (Month, Year) / I RESIDED CONTINUOUSLY IN THE U.S. From (Mo., Yr.) To (Mo., Yr.) / DATE NATURALIZATION (Mo., Day, Yr.) / PLACE

21. DO NOT SIGN APPLICATION UNTIL REQUESTED TO DO SO BY PERSON ADMINISTERING OATH
I have not, since acquiring United States citizenship, performed any of the acts listed under "Acts or Conditions" on the reverse of this application form (unless explanatory statement is attached). I solemnly swear (or affirm) that the statements made on this application are true and the photograph attached is a true likeness of me.

Subscribed and sworn to (affirmed) before me
Month Day Year
PLACE OF ISSUE (SEAL)
☐ Clerk of Court or
☐ PASSPORT Agent
☐ Postal Employee
☐ (Vice) Consul USA At _____
X _____
(Sign in presence of person authorized to accept application)
(Signature of person authorized to accept application)

22. APPLICANT'S IDENTIFYING DOCUMENTS ☐ PASSPORT ☐ DRIVER'S LICENSE ☐ OTHER (Specify)
ISSUE DATE Month Day Year / EXPIRATION DATE Month Day Year
PLACE OF ISSUE
No.
ISSUED IN THE NAME OF

24. FOR ISSUING OFFICE USE ONLY (Applicant's evidence of citizenship)
☐ Birth Cert. SR CR City Filed/Issued:
☐ Passport Bearer's Name:
☐ Report of Birth
☐ Naturalization/Citizenship Cert. No.:
☐ Other:
☐ Seen & Returned
☐ Attached

APPLICATION APPROVAL
Examiner Name
Office, Date

24. FEE _____ EXEC. _____ POST _____

FORM DSP-11 (12-87) (SEE INSTRUCTIONS ON REVERSE) Form Approved OMB No. 1405-0004 (Exp. 8/1/89)

know and cannot find out any of this information, write "Unknown" or leave the space blank.

12. Write your mother's full maiden name (first and last names). Then write the country where she was born and the month, day, and year she was born (all in numbers). Also check whether or not she is a U.S. citizen. If you do not know and cannot find out any of this information, write "Unknown" or leave the space blank.

13. This box relates to your travel plans. On the left side of the box, write the name of the country or countries you plan to visit. Write the date (all in numbers) you plan to go to the first country you will visit. If you are not sure of the date, write a month rather than a specific date. Finally, write how long your trip will be.

14. This section of the form is for people who have had U.S. passports before. If you have never had one, check the No box and move to the next section of the form. If you have had a passport before, check Yes and answer the other questions in this section. If you have your passport with you, check the Submitted box and move on to next section of the form. If you once had a passport and you no longer have it, you must answer the rest of the questions. Write the name in which the passport was issued, the number (if you know it), and the date it was issued (if you know it). Under Disposition, briefly explain what happened to the passport.

15. Your photograph will go here. The passport agent will attach the photo, so you do not have to do anything or write anything here.

16. If you have never been married, check the No box and move on to the next section of the form. If you are now married or have been married in the past, complete the questions that apply to you. Be sure to write the dates all in numbers. If you are widowed or divorced, the date requested is the date your spouse died or the date your divorce became final.

17. This section of the application requests the name, address, and phone number of someone not traveling with you who should be contacted in case of emergency. Although the form states that you do not have to provide this information, it is a good idea to provide it anyway.

18. Only naturalized citizens have to answer questions in this section. If you are not a naturalized citizen, go on to the next section. If you are a naturalized citizen, provide the information requested.

19. You will be asked to sign this section of the form after the passport agent administers an oath. The conditions in the oath

are written on the back of the application, and you should read them before you sign. The passport agent will fill out the left part of this form. You will write your signature on the right side.

20. The passport agent will fill out the rest of the form. Do not write anything in these sections.

Fill Out the Application

Even if you already have a passport, fill out the application using your own personal information. If you are not a U. S. citizen, fill out as much of this form as you can and leave the rest blank.

LESSON 29

Voter Registration

Every citizen of the United States over the age of 18 has the right to vote in local, state, and federal elections. Many people believe that voting is more than just a right; it is a responsibility of all citizens.

In order for you to vote, you must first register with your local board of elections. You can get a voter registration form from your county board of elections or from the local branch of the League of Women Voters. The addresses and phone numbers for both are in the phone book. In many states, you can request the form by mail and return it by mail as well. So you do not need to register in person.

During major election years (such as during a presidential election year), different citizens' groups hold voter registration drives. These drives are intended to encourage people to register to vote. During these times, you may find voter registration forms at shopping centers, malls, or even on busy street corners.

In order to vote, a person must be a citizen and be over 18 years of age. In addition, some states have residency requirements for voters. This means that you must live at your present address for a certain amount of time, such as 30 days, before you can vote. If you do not meet this requirement but you want to vote, contact the board of elections. You may be able to register anyhow.

Many states may also require that you register a certain number of days before a general election. The amount of time may be 25 to 30 days.

If you once registered but have not voted in more than five years, you will have to register again in order to vote in a current election.

▶ Be Prepared

You do not need much in the way of preparation to fill out a voter registration form. You need to know how long you have lived at your present address. If you registered before, you should know where you lived at that time and when you registered. If you are a naturalized citizen, you must know where and when your naturalization papers were issued.

Voter Registration Form Vocabulary

affidavit   A sworn statement.

affirm   State as true.

enrollment   Registration.

perjury Swearing to something that is not true.

primary An election that selects candidates for a political party.

residence The place where you live.

spouse Husband or wife.

▸ How to Fill Out the Form

The following hints will help you fill out the form. The numbers in the following list match the circled numbers on the form. Some parts of the form do not have circled numbers. You should be able to fill out these parts of the form without any special hints or explanation.

1. Write the initial of your middle name.

2. If you use *Jr.* or *Sr.* as part of your name, write the one that applies to you. If you use numbers with your name, such as John Smith III (John Smith the third), write the number here even though the box says Jr. or Sr.

3. If you use a post office box to receive your mail, do not write that here. At this place on the form, you should write the address of the place where you live, not where you receive your mail.

4. If the address where you receive your mail is different from the address of the place where you live, write the mailing address here. For example, you might write your post office box number here. If you receive your mail at the address where you live, do not write anything in this box.

5. Write your birth date all in numbers. For example, if your birth date is October 22, 1970, write "10 22 70."

6. Write your telephone number, including area code. You do not have to provide your phone number here if you have an unlisted number. An **unlisted number** does not appear in the phone book. This is because the person who has the number does not want it listed in the phone book.

7. This question asks how long you have lived at your current address. There are places for you to write the number of years, months, and days. If you have lived in the same place for a long time, you probably do not know the number of days or months. In this case, it is OK to write only the number of years or the years and months.

8. You will have to write very small to fit in your employer's name and full address (street address plus city, state, and zip code) in this space. Abbreviate as much as possible so that you can fit everything. Write "St." for street, "Ave." for avenue, "E." for east, "Co." for company, and so forth.

LESSON 30 VOTER REGISTRATION

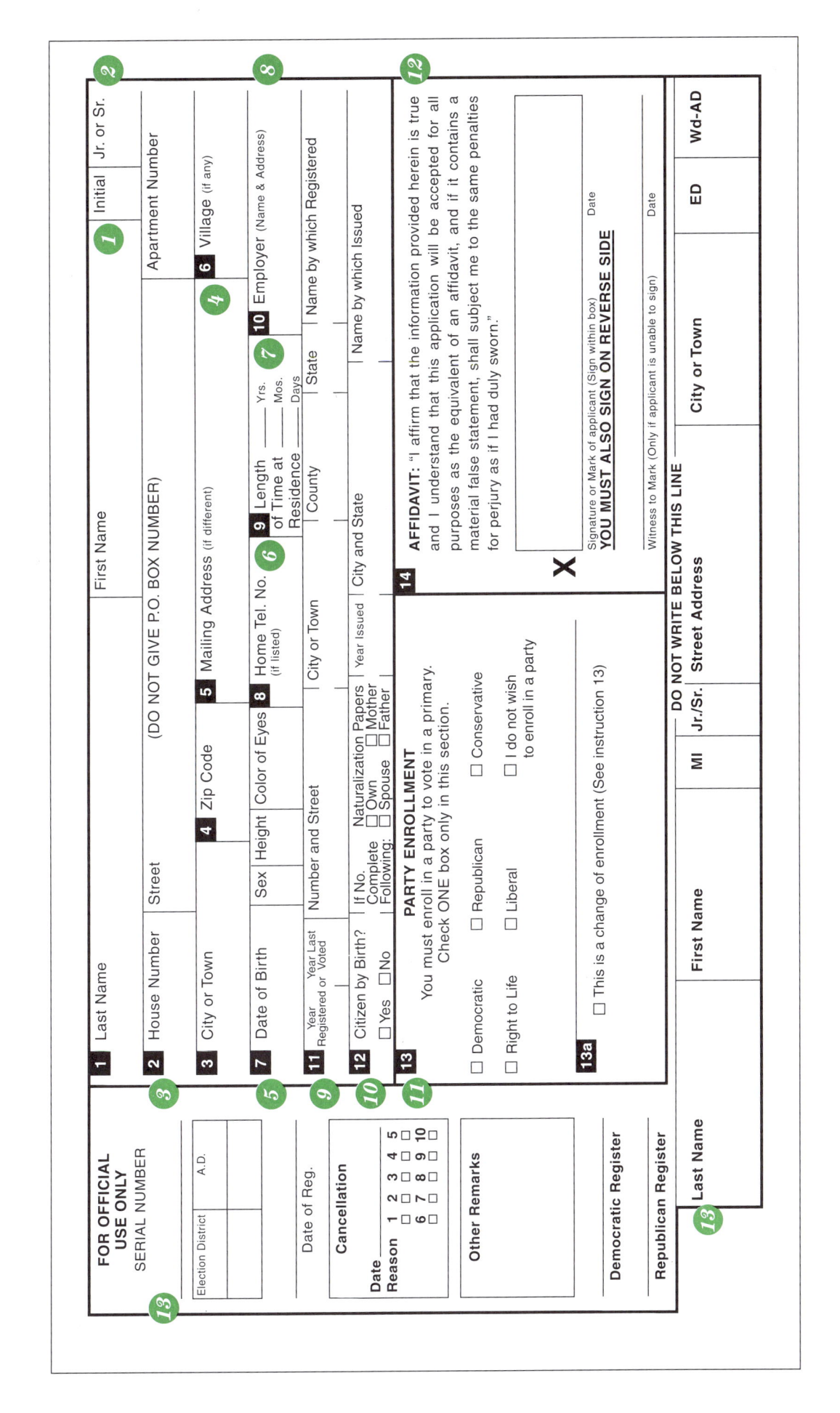

9. This whole line of the form relates to people who have registered before and must register again. If you have not registered before, you can skip this line and go on to the next one.

   If you are reregistering, you must answer the questions on this line. If you are not sure of the exact year you last registered or voted, you can guess or you can put question marks in these boxes. You should be able to fill out the other questions on this line without any problems. They ask where you lived when you registered before and the name you had at that time.

10. This line is about citizenship. If you were born a citizen of the United States, check the *Yes* box and go on to the next question. If you were not born a citizen, answer the rest of the questions on this line.

11. You can enroll in one of the political parties listed on the form. Enrolling in a party means that you will be allowed to vote in the primary elections for that party. Enrolling in a party does not mean that you have to vote for the candidates of that party in the general election. If you prefer not to enroll in a political party, check the correct box.

12. When you sign this form, you are swearing that all the information you provided on the form is true. It is against the law to provide false information on this form. Sign the form and write the date all in numbers.

    A person who cannot write can place a mark in place of his or her signature. In this case, someone must witness that the person registering made the mark. The witness must sign and date the form.

    There is a place on the back of the form where you will also sign.

13. Do not write anything in these places.

Fill Out the Form

Even if you have already registered to vote or if you are not eligible to vote, use your own personal information and fill out the form.

LESSON 30

Income Tax Return (FORM 1040EZ)

In the United States, you must pay federal income taxes and social security taxes on money that you earn in one calendar year. Even if you earn a small amount of money, you will have to file an income tax return.

Some states and cities also require that you pay income taxes each year.

Income tax returns are filed in the calendar year following the year in which you earned money. For example, if you worked in 1993, you will file your 1993 tax return in 1994.

Taxpayers are given until April 15 to file their tax returns. If people need more time, they can ask for an **extension**, which gives them a few more months to file their returns. If you do not have an extension and do not file your return by April 15, the government will charge you a penalty for being late.

Although some people wait until the last minute, it is best to file your tax return as soon as you can.

▸ *Be Prepared*

Before you can file your tax return, you must collect certain information and wait to receive certain forms in the mail.

If you have filed tax returns in previous years, the government will send you the correct forms and an information booklet. If you have not filed tax returns before, you can call your local IRS office. They will tell you what forms you need and send them to you. Or you can get the forms at the post office.

The company or companies you worked for during the year will send you a **W-2 form**. This form is filled out by the company. It states how much money you earned during the year and how much money in taxes was deducted from your paycheck for the whole year. (A W-2 form is shown later in this lesson.)

You receive several copies of the W-2. You keep one copy and attach one copy to each tax return. For example, one copy is for your federal tax return. You would attach another copy to your state tax return if the state in which you live has an income tax. You cannot figure your taxes and mail the return until the W-2 form arrives in the mail.

You may have a savings account or some other form of investment for which you are paid interest. If so, the bank or company with which you have the investment will send you a statement of how much interest you earned for the year. The interest is considered part of your annual income, so you cannot file your tax return until you receive a statement from the bank or company.

It is possible to use a very simple tax return form, such as the one shown later in this lesson. In order to use this form, you must be single and not have any dependents. If you use this simple form, all you need to file the return is what has already been mentioned.

Some people must file longer, more complicated returns. For their income taxes, these people must use information and records that have piled up during the year. The following list gives examples of some of these records.

- *Medical expenses.* Sometimes, people can deduct their medical expenses from their taxes. This means that they do not have to pay tax on some or all of the money they used for medical expenses. Medical expenses include such things as doctor bills, dentist bills, bills for eyeglasses, bills for prescription medication, and hospital bills. People who can deduct medical expenses from their taxes need receipts or copies of the paid bills, so they need to save these records throughout the year.
- *Business expenses.* Some people spend money for business reasons. Some or all of these expenses can be deducted from their taxes. Receipts are needed for all business expenses.
- *Charitable contributions.* If people give money to charities during the year, they can deduct the amounts they gave from their taxes. Again, they will need receipts.

When people who have expenses are ready to do their taxes, they add up their expenses for the year and write the information on a tax form. The form they use is different from the one shown in this book. If you are not sure which tax form to use, you can often tell from the form you used the previous year. If your finances have not changed much from the previous year, you can probably use the same form.

Some people find income tax returns very hard to fill out. If you are not sure what you should do or feel uncomfortable about filling out the return yourself, you can pay someone to fill it out for you. Accountants and companies that specialize in taxes are available. Some companies are located in malls, shopping areas, and storefronts. The amount they charge usually depends upon the number of tax forms that are needed. This often does not amount to a lot of money.

The form shown in this book is very easy to fill out.

Income Tax Return Vocabulary

adjusted gross income The total of all the money earned as payment for work and interest.

dependents People who rely on you for financial support.

IRS   Abbreviation for *Internal Revenue Service*, which is the part of the federal government in charge of income taxes.

perjury   Swearing to something that is not true.

refund   An amount of money returned. In this case, a refund is the money you may get back from the government.

salary   A fixed amount of money paid for work performed. A salary is usually determined on a yearly basis.

taxable income   The total amount of money on which you must pay taxes.

taxable interest income   Money that is earned from savings or investments on which taxes must be paid. Some investments are tax-free.

wages   Payment of money for work done. Wages are usually determined on an hourly, weekly, or piecework basis.

How to Fill Out an Income Tax Return

Information about who should fill out the 1040EZ form and instructions for filling out the form are printed on the front and the back of the form, both of which are shown later in this lesson. This form is called EZ because it is "easy" to fill out. When it is sent to you in the mail, it comes with an instruction booklet. However, you will not need the booklet here.

Read the information and instructions before you begin to fill out the form. All the page numbers mentioned on the 1040EZ form refer to pages in the instruction booklet. You can ignore the page numbers in this lesson.

The following hints will help you fill out the income tax return. The numbers in the following list match the circled numbers on the form.

1. When you receive tax forms in the mail, a label with your name and address is included. Since you do not have the label in this lesson, write the information requested.

2. The reason numbers are printed here is to show you how the numbers you write should look. You do not have to write anything here.

3. Write each number of your social security number in each of the boxes.

4. The money ($1) you donate to a presidential campaign fund decreases the amount of money that candidates must raise on their own. Your money does not go to a specific candidate. If you want to donate $1, check the Yes box. If you do not, check the No box.

5. Write the total amount you received for the year in wages, salaries, and tips. The amount of wages or salaries will be printed on the W-2 form. Even if you do not have a W-2 form for all the money you earned, you must report it all. Write the amount so that each number of the amount is printed in each of the boxes. You do not have to attach the W-2 form until after you have finished filling out the form.

6. If you earned interest on a savings account or some other kind of investment, write the total amount of all the interest you earned. You must use another tax form if the amount of interest you earned is more than $400.

7. Write the total of the two numbers you added.

8. Assume here that you cannot be claimed on someone else's taxes. Check the No box and write the amount 5,900 in the boxes.

9. Write the answer you get by subtracting.

10. Look at your W-2 form and find the amount that was withheld (deducted) from the money you earned. If you have more than one W-2 form, add the amounts withheld. Write the total amount in the boxes.

11. The tax tables show how much money you should pay in taxes based on your taxable income. To find the right number on the tax table, look at the amount you wrote on line 5 of the form (item 9 in this list). Then follow the headings on the tax table. For example, if line 5 is $26,390, first find the heading that applies to $26,000. Then read down the column until you come to the

If line 35 (taxable income) is—		And you are—			
At least	But less than	Single	Married filing jointly *	Married filing separately	Head of a household
			Your tax is—		
26,000						
26,000	26,050	4,499	3,904	4,960	3,904
26,050	26,100	4,513	3,911	4,974	3,911
26,100	26,150	4,527	3,919	4,988	3,919
26,150	26,200	4,541	3,926	5,002	3,926
26,200	26,250	4,555	3,934	5,016	3,934
26,250	26,300	4,569	3,941	5,030	3,941
26,300	26,350	4,583	3,949	5,044	3,949
26,350	26,400	4,597	3,956	5,058	3,956
26,400	26,450	4,611	3,964	5,072	3,964
26,450	26,500	4,625	3,971	5,086	3,971
26,500	26,550	4,639	3,979	5,100	3,979
26,550	26,600	4,653	3,986	5,114	3,986
26,600	26,650	4,667	3,994	5,128	3,994
26,650	26,700	4,681	4,001	5,142	4,001
26,700	26,750	4,695	4,009	5,156	4,009
26,750	26,800	4,709	4,016	5,170	4,016
26,800	26,850	4,723	4,024	5,184	4,024
26,850	26,900	4,737	4,031	5,198	4,031
26,900	26,950	4,751	4,039	5,212	4,039
26,950	27,000	4,765	4,046	5,226	4,046

line that has 2 amounts that $26,390 falls between. Then read the columns to the right. For the 1040EZ, you must be single, so find the amount for a single person. This is the amount of taxes you should have paid based on the amount you earned. Find the amount that is right for your earnings and write the amount in the boxes.

12. If the amount on line 6 of the form is more than the amount on line 7, subtract the amount on line 7 from the amount on line 6 and write the amount in the boxes. This is the amount of money the government owes you. If the amount on line 6 is smaller than the amount on line 7, do not write anything.

13. If the amount on line 7 of the form is more than the amount on line 6, subtract the amount on line 6 from the amount on line 7 and write the answer in the boxes. This is the amount you owe the government. You must send the government a check or money order for this amount. Follow the instructions for filling out the check or money order. You must include the amount you owe when you mail the income tax return.

14. Sign your name after the *X*. Write today's date all in numbers. For example, if the date is March 12, 1993, you would write "3/12/93." Then write your job title.

Fill Out the Income Tax Return

Below is a W-2 form, which shows all the money you earned for the year and the amount of taxes withheld from the amount you earned. In addition, you earned $291.26 from interest on your savings account. You cannot be claimed on someone else's taxes.

1 Control number 4271	22222	For Paperwork Reduction Act Notice, see back of Copy D. OMB NO. 1545-0008	For Official Use Only	
2 Employer's name, address, and ZIP code Eastern Graphics, Inc. 128 Elm Street Alexandria, VA 22341		3 Employer's identification number 29,4321672	4 Employer's State number	
		5 Stat. employee / Deceased / Legal rep. / 942 emp. / Subtotal		Void
		6 Allocated tips	7 Advance EIC payment	
8 Employee's social security number 175-28-1963	9 Federal income tax withheld 4,382	10 Wages, tips, other compensation 23,920	11 Social security tax withheld 2,395	
12 Employee's name (first, middle, last) Margaret O'Connell 41 Hilltop Road Alexandria, VA 22311 15 Employee's address and ZIP code		13 Social security wages	14 Social security tips	
		16 •		
		17 State income tax	18 State wages, tips, etc.	19 Name of State
		20 Local income tax	21 Local wages, tips, etc.	22 Name of locality

Form **W-2 Wage and Tax Statement 19**—

Copy A For Social Security Administration
• See Instructions for Forms W–2 and W–2P

Department of the Treasury
Internal Revenue Service

Do NOT Cut or Separate Forms on This Page

Assume that you are single, that you have no dependents, and that you are not claimed as a dependent by someone else. Fill out the income tax return, using your own name and address and the information provided. Use the tax tables below.

1992 Tax Table—Continued

If line 35 (taxable income) is—		And you are—				If line 35 (taxable income) is—		And you are—			
At least	But less than	Single	Married filing jointly *	Married filing separately	Head of a household	At least	But less than	Single	Married filing jointly *	Married filing separately	Head of a household
		Your tax is—						Your tax is—			

14,000

14,000	14,050	2,104	2,104	2,104	2,104
14,050	14,100	2,111	2,111	2,111	2,111
14,100	14,150	2,119	2,119	2,119	2,119
14,150	14,200	2,126	2,126	2,126	2,126
14,200	14,250	2,134	2,134	2,134	2,134
14,250	14,300	2,141	2,141	2,141	2,141
14,300	14,350	2,149	2,149	2,149	2,149
14,350	14,400	2,156	2,156	2,156	2,156
14,400	14,450	2,164	2,164	2,164	2,164
14,450	14,500	2,171	2,171	2,171	2,171
14,500	14,550	2,179	2,179	2,179	2,179
14,550	14,600	2,186	2,186	2,186	2,186
14,600	14,650	2,194	2,194	2,194	2,194
14,650	14,700	2,201	2,201	2,201	2,201
14,700	14,750	2,209	2,209	2,209	2,209
14,750	14,800	2,216	2,216	2,216	2,216
14,800	14,850	2,224	2,224	2,224	2,224
14,850	14,900	2,231	2,231	2,231	2,231
14,900	14,950	2,239	2,239	2,239	2,239
14,950	15,000	2,246	2,246	2,246	2,246

15,000

15,000	15,050	2,254	2,254	2,254	2,254
15,050	15,100	2,261	2,261	2,261	2,261
15,100	15,150	2,269	2,269	2,269	2,269
15,150	15,200	2,276	2,276	2,276	2,276
15,200	15,250	2,284	2,284	2,284	2,284
15,250	15,300	2,291	2,291	2,291	2,291
15,300	15,350	2,299	2,299	2,299	2,299
15,350	15,400	2,306	2,306	2,306	2,306
15,400	15,450	2,314	2,314	2,314	2,314
15,450	15,500	2,321	2,321	2,321	2,321
15,500	15,550	2,329	2,329	2,329	2,329
15,550	15,600	2,336	2,336	2,336	2,336
15,600	15,650	2,344	2,344	2,344	2,344
15,650	15,700	2,351	2,351	2,351	2,351
15,700	15,750	2,359	2,359	2,359	2,359
15,750	15,800	2,366	2,366	2,366	2,366
15,800	15,850	2,374	2,374	2,374	2,374
15,850	15,900	2,381	2,381	2,381	2,381
15,900	15,950	2,389	2,389	2,389	2,389
15,950	16,000	2,396	2,396	2,396	2,396

17,000

17,000	17,050	2,554	2,554	2,554	2,554
17,050	17,100	2,561	2,561	2,561	2,561
17,100	17,150	2,569	2,569	2,569	2,569
17,150	17,200	2,576	2,576	2,576	2,576
17,200	17,250	2,584	2,584	2,584	2,584
17,250	17,300	2,591	2,591	2,591	2,591
17,300	17,350	2,599	2,599	2,599	2,599
17,350	17,400	2,606	2,606	2,606	2,606
17,400	17,450	2,614	2,614	2,614	2,614
17,450	17,500	2,621	2,621	2,621	2,621
17,500	17,550	2,629	2,629	2,629	2,269
17,550	17,600	2,636	2,636	2,636	2,636
17,600	17,650	2,644	2,644	2,644	2,644
17,650	17,700	2,651	2,651	2,651	2,651
17,700	17,750	2,659	2,659	2,659	2,659
17,750	17,800	2,666	2,666	2,666	2,666
17,800	17,850	2,674	2,674	2,674	2,674
17,850	17,900	2,681	2,681	2,681	2,681
17,900	17,950	2,689	2,689	2,692	2,689
17,950	18,000	2,696	2,696	2,706	2,696

18,000

18,000	18,050	2,704	2,704	2,720	2,704
18,050	18,100	2,711	2,711	2,734	2,711
18,100	18,150	2,719	2,719	2,748	2,719
18,150	18,200	2,726	2,726	2,762	2,726
18,200	18,250	2,734	2,734	2,776	2,734
18,250	18,300	2,741	2,741	2,790	2,741
18,300	18,350	2,749	2,749	2,804	2,749
18,350	18,400	2,756	2,756	2,818	2,756
18,400	18,450	2,764	2,764	2,832	2,764
18,450	18,500	2,771	2,771	2,846	2,771
18,500	18,550	2,779	2,779	2,860	2,779
18,550	18,600	2,786	2,786	2,874	2,786
18,600	18,650	2,794	2,794	2,888	2,794
18,650	18,700	2,801	2,801	2,902	2,801
18,700	18,750	2,809	2,809	2,916	2,809
18,750	18,800	2,816	2,816	2,930	2,816
18,800	18,850	2,824	2,824	2,944	2,824
18,850	18,900	2,831	2,831	2,958	2,831
18,900	18,950	2,839	2,839	2,972	2,839
18,950	19,000	2,846	2,846	2,986	2,846

Form **1040EZ**

Department of the Treasury—Internal Revenue Service
Income Tax Return for Single Filers With No Dependents (B) **1992**

Name & address

① Use the **IRS label** (see page 10). If you don't have one, please print.

- Print your name (first, initial, last)
- Home address (number and street. If you have a P.O. box, see page 10.) Apt. no.
- City, town or post office, state, and ZIP code. If you have a foreign address, see page 10.

② Please print your numbers like this:
9 8 7 6 5 4 3 2 1 0

③ Your social security number

Please see instructions on the back. Also, see the Form 1040EZ booklet.

Presidential Election Campaign (See page 10). Do you want $1 to go to this fund?

Note: *Checking "Yes" will not change your tax or reduce your refund.*

④ Yes No

Dollars   Cents

Report your income

Attach Copy B of Form(s) W-2 here. Attach tax payment on top of Form(s) W-2.

Note: *You **must** check Yes or No.*

1 Total wages, salaries, and tips. This should be shown in box 10 of your W-2 form(s). Attach your W-2 form(s). 1   ⑤

2 Taxable interest income of $400 or less. If the total is more than $400, you cannot use Form 1040EZ. 2   ⑥

3 Add lines 1 and 2. This is your **adjusted gross income.** 3   ⑦

4 Can your parents (or someone else) claim you on their return?
☐ **Yes.** Do worksheet on back; enter amount from line E here.
☐ **No.** Enter 5,900.00 This is the total of your standard deduction and personal exemption. 4   ⑧

5 Subtract line 4 from line 3. If line 4 is larger than line 3, enter 0. This is your **taxable income.** 5   ⑨

Figure your tax

6 Enter your Federal income tax withheld from box 9 of your W-2 form(s). 6   ⑩

7 **Tax.** Look at line 5 above. Use the amount on **line 5** to find your tax in the tax table on pages 22-24 of the booklet. Then, enter the tax from the table on this line. 7   ⑪

Refund or amount you owe

8 If line 6 is larger than line 7, subtract line 7 from line 6. This is your **refund.** 8   ⑫

9 If line 7 is larger than line 6, subtract line 6 from line 7. This is the **amount you owe.** Attach your payment for full amount payable to the "Internal Revenue Service." Write your name, address, social security number, daytime phone number, and "1992 Form 1040EZ" on it. 9   ⑬

Sign your return

Keep a copy of this form for your records.

I have read this return. Under penalties of perjury, I declare that to the best of my knowledge and belief, the return is true, correct, and complete.

Your signature   Date
X   Your occupation   ⑭

For IRS use Only—Please do not write in boxes below.

For Privacy Act and Paperwork Reduction Act Notice, see page 4 in the booklet.

Form 1040EZ (1992)

1992 Instructions for Form 1040EZ

Use this form if
- Your filing status is single.
- You do not claim any dependents.
- You had **only** wages, salaries, tips, and taxable scholarship or fellowship grants, and your taxable interest income was $400 or less. **Caution:** *If you earned tips, including allocated tips, that are not included in box 13 and box 14 of your W-2, you may not be able to use Form 1040EZ. See page 12 in the booklet. Also, you cannot use this form if you had more than one employer and your total wages were over $55,500.*
- You did not receive any advance earned income credit payments.
- You were under 65* and not blind at the end of 1992.
- Your taxable income (line 5) is less than $50,000.

* *If you turned 65 on January 1, 1993, you are considered to be age 65 at the end of 1992.*

If you are not sure about your filing status, see page 6 in the booklet. If you have questions about dependents, see Tele-Tax (topic no. 155) on page 20 in the booklet.

If you can't use this form, see Tele-Tax (topic no. 152) on page 20 in the booklet.

Filling in your return

Please print your numbers inside the boxes. Do not type your numbers. Do not use dollar signs.

Most people can fill in the form by following the instructions on the front. But you will have to use the booklet if you received a scholarship or fellowship grant or tax-exempt interest income, such as on municipal bonds. Also, use the booklet if you received a Form 1099-INT showing income tax withheld (backup withholding).

Remember, you must report your wages, salaries, and tips even if you don't get a W-2 form from your employer. You must also report all your taxable interest income, including interest from savings accounts at banks, savings and loans, credit unions, etc., even if you don't get a Form 1099-INT.

If you paid someone to prepare your return, that person must also sign it and show other information. See page 15 in the booklet.

Standard deduction worksheet for dependents who checked "Yes" on line 4

Fill in this worksheet to figure the amount to enter on line 4 if someone can claim you as a dependent, even if that person chooses not to claim you. To find out if someone can claim you as a dependent, see Tele-Tax (topic no. 155) on page 20 in the booklet.

A. Enter the amount from line 1 on the front.	A.	_____
B. Minimum amount.	B.	600.00
C. Look at lines A and B above. Enter the LARGER of the two amounts here.	C.	_____
D. Maximum amount.	D.	3,600.00
E. Look at lines C and D above. Enter the SMALLER of the two amounts here and on line 4 on the front.	E.	_____

If you checked "No" because no one can claim you as a dependent, enter 5,900.00 on line 4. This is the total of your standard deduction (3,600.00) and personal exemption (2,300.00).

Avoid common mistakes

This checklist is to help you make sure your form is filled in correctly.

1. Did you check your computations (additions, subtractions, etc.) especially when figuring your taxable income, Federal income tax withheld, and your refund or amount you owe?
2. Did you check the "Yes" box on line 4 if your parents (or someone else) can claim you as a dependent on their 1992 return, even if they choose not to claim you? If no one can claim you as a dependent, did you check the "No" box?
3. Did you enter an amount on line 4? If you checked the "Yes" box on line 4, did you fill in the worksheet above to figure the amount to enter? If you checked the "No" box, did you enter 5,900.00?
4. Did you use the amount from **line 5** to find your tax in the table? Did you enter the correct tax on line 7?
5. If you didn't get a label, did you enter your name, address (including ZIP code), and social security number in the spaces provided on Form 1040EZ?
6. If you got a label, does it show your correct name, address, and social security number? If not, did you enter the correct information?
7. Did you attach your W-2 forms(s) to the left margin of your return? And did you sign and date Form 1040EZ and enter your occupation?

Mailing your return

Mail your return by **April 15, 1993**. Use the envelope that came with your booklet. If you don't have that envelope, see page 25 in the booklet for the address to use.